The
Workbook
on
Virtues
& the
Fruit
of the
Spirit

Maxie Dunnam and
Kimberly Dunnam Reisman

UPPER
ROOM BOOKS
NASHVILLE

The Workbook on Virtues and the Fruit of the Spirit

Cover Transparency: Gianni Dagli Orti/Corbis
Cover Design: John Robinson
Interior Design: Charles Sutherland
Second Printing: 1999

The Upper Room Web Site: http://www.upperroom.org

The Library of Congress Cataloging-in-Publication Data

Dunnam, Maxie D.
  The workbook on virtues and the fruit of the spirit/by Maxie Dunnam and Kimberly Dunnam Reisman.
       p.   cm.
  ISBN 0-8358-0854-8
  1. Cardinal virtues—Prayer-books and devotions—English. 2. Virtues—Prayer-books and devotions—English. 3. Fruit of the Spirit—Prayer-books and devotions—English. 4. Devotional calendars. 5. Retreats. I. Reisman, Kimberly Dunnam, 1960-   . II. Title.
  BV4645.D85 1998
  214'.4—dc21   98-17290
                                                                        CIP

Printed in the United States of America

With love and admiration
to John and Jane Reisman, in-laws, and friends
who through their commitment
have shown God's grace
active in the world.

CONTENTS

INTRODUCTION / 7

WEEK ONE / 13
Predicament and Promise

WEEK TWO / 31
Wisdom and Courage

WEEK THREE / 55
Justice and Temperance

WEEK FOUR / 79
The Theological Virtues: Faith and Hope

WEEK FIVE / 101
The Fruit of the Spirit: Love

WEEK SIX / 123
Joy and Peace

WEEK SEVEN / 145
Patience/Kindness/Goodness

WEEK EIGHT / 167
Faithfulness/Gentleness/Self-control

BIBLIOGRAPHY / 188

AFFIRMATION CARDS / 191

In popular culture and within the faith community, every era seems to have its own emphasis. There have been times during the twentieth century when the issues of sin and virtue have been accentuated in discussions of the challenges and difficulties of our society. More often than not, however, as the decades progressed, our emphasis changed. Discussions of sin were either avoided altogether or replaced, for instance, by debates about sickness or the quality of living environments. The same has been true of the idea of virtue. Rather than focusing on the value of developing our moral selves, we have often over the years avoided the subject completely, seeming to assume that moral virtue was too priggish a notion to be helpful. At other times we have taken a more relativistic stance, asserting that moral virtue is not an objective reality that can be particularized to differing conditions but is instead circumstantial or situational.

More recently, there have been periods where we tried to have it both ways. Uncomfortable with direct discussions of the importance of developing our moral selves, yet not wanting to avoid it entirely, we have put enormous energy into exploring such vague and amorphous ideas as "self-actualization" or "fully actualizing our potential." The 1990s, however, have seen a renewed interest and focus on the idea of virtue and the significance of developing moral values. Just a cursory glance at the Library of Congress's Internet home page reveals more than eighty-five titles published since 1990 alone. These titles, located simply by using the word "virtue" as the subject, were as diverse in content as *Pagan Virtue: An Essay in Ethics* by John Casey and *Christian Virtues in Medical Practice* by Edmund D. Pellegrino and David C. Thomasma, not to mention William J. Bennett's bestseller, *The Book of Virtues*, or Dan Quayle and Diane Medved's *The American Family: Discovering the Values That Make Us Strong*.

We hope that such attention to the concept of virtue indicates a recognition of the importance of weaving a strong moral fabric for our lives. Like society as a whole, each of us as individuals is both attracted to and repelled by the idea of developing moral virtue. We want to be good, but aren't always able. We don't completely like being bad, but sometimes don't mind it. This battle has been with us from the beginning, as has the debate over the entire issue of goodness itself. There have been those who have questioned whether goodness is really good or whether goodness is real at all. Moral cynicism asserts that the struggle is not between good and evil but simply the push and pull of power. Pragmatism, or moral relativism, puts forth that the issue is not what is good or what is bad but what works and what doesn't. And, as we have seen in the last half of the twentieth century particularly, the influence of psychology has shifted the issue to simply healthy or not healthy.

As Christians seeking to find a resolution to the struggle we feel within us, we must first remember whose we are. We belong to a God who created each of us as one good, whole self. Granted, somewhere along the way something happened to that good, whole self, obscuring the wholeness in fragmentation and estrangement, and making the goodness supremely vulnerable and responsive to the presence of evil. Yet, our freedom to choose has always remained. God did not create us to be puppets or robots, but God desires that we choose freely—just as God freely chose to create us in the first place. Therefore, we do not have to succumb to our inner responsiveness to evil. We can remember that "God saw everything that God was made, and indeed, it was very good" (Gen. 1:31). We are always free to choose to be the good self God created us to be or to become captivated by the evil that is all around us.

There are those who would respond to the idea of freely choosing the good with the question of whether goodness is even possible at all. We believe it is. We do not believe that it is easy, but it is possible. It is possible because God has not abandoned us. On the contrary, God has been seeking to be in relationship with us since the moment we first turned away. In seeking to be in relationship, God offers us the tools we need to turn away from the presence of evil and toward our created purpose: goodness.

This workbook explores the tools available for us as we strive to be the good selves God created us to be. While there are many tools that we could name, we have focused on what has, over the course of time, come to be known as the seven cardinal virtues. Seven has always been a significant spiritual number: there were seven days of creation and seven days of the week. Thus, by the fourth century a list of seven tools for the moral life had been created and called the cardinal virtues. It was not that there were no other tools for character-building; rather, these were seen to be the cream of the crop. They are wisdom (prudence), courage (fortitude), justice, temperance, faith, hope, and love.

The word *virtue* comes first from the Greek word *arete* which means "power." This is a major hint in answering the question "Is goodness possible?" God not only gives us tools in the virtues, God gives us power. The virtues show God's power of goodness within us. They are the evidence of God's love, of God's grace. The first four virtues (wisdom, courage, justice, and temperance) are known as the classical or natural virtues. These virtues existed long before Christianity came into being and are evidence of God's natural grace that is offered as a gift to all humanity. The remaining three virtues (faith, hope, and love) are known as the "theological virtues" because they reflect a particular aspect of God's grace, given as a gift through our relationship with God through Israel and Christ. Not only will we look at the seven cardinal virtues, we will also consider the "fruit of the Spirit" named by Paul in Galatians 5.

Thomas Aquinas was one of the great champions of developing the virtues in our moral life. He described the two sides of virtue: power and habit. The virtues were a source of power in developing our character because they were God's gifts of grace to us. Therefore, we had access to them and the power to develop them because God had provided all of that for us. Aquinas also considered the virtues to be habits. Like all habits, good and bad, they developed through repetition and exercise. Therefore, through the power of God's grace in the virtues, and our own disciplined exercise of them, we are able to strengthen our characters and move toward the good selves God created us to be. So, like Aquinas, we believe that living a life of moral virtue is possible, though not without God's help.

Serious study of the virtues is the process of seeking God's help in order to be the best we can be: the responsible, whole, and good self God created. It is our prayer that you will use this workbook as a guidepost as you journey toward your created purpose. As you study, remember that we receive the virtues as gifts from God for power. This knowledge gives us confidence. Remember also that virtues are habits to be exercised through training and discipline. This knowledge provides us a challenge. Finally, remember that virtue does not develop in a vacuum. It is nurtured through purposeful communities that treasure virtue, whose vocation is to teach and live the moral life. While this workbook may be helpful on a personal level, our striving for the moral life will not be consistently fruitful without the support of a morally serious community that can provide reinforcement and guidance.

The Plan

This workbook is designed for individual and group use. Let's look at the process. It is simple but very important.

We have learned from years of teaching and ministry with small groups that a six- to-eight-week period for a group study is the most manageable and effective. Also, we have learned that persons can best appropriate content and truth in small doses. That is the reason for organizing the material in segments to be read daily.

The plan for this workbook is the same as for the previous ones we have written. It calls for an eight-week commitment. You are asked to give about thirty minutes each day to reflect on some aspect of virtue and how it can express itself in your life. For most persons, the thirty minutes will come at the beginning of the day. However, if it is not possible for you to give the time at the beginning of the day, do it whenever the time is available, but do it regularly. This is not only an intellectual pursuit, though it is that, it is a spiritual journey, the purpose of which is to incorporate the content into your daily life.

It is a personal journey, but our hope is that you will share it with some fellow pilgrims who will meet together once each week during the eight weeks of the study.

The workbook is arranged into eight major divisions, each designed to guide you for one week. These divisions contain seven sections, one for each day of the week. Each day of the week will have three major aspects: reading, reflecting and recording ideas and thoughts about the material and your own understanding and experience, and some practical suggestions for incorporating ideas from the reading material into your daily life.

In each day's section, you will read something about virtue and its productive possibilities for your life. It won't be too much to read, but it will be enough to challenge thought and action.

Quotations from most sources other than scripture are followed by the author's name and page number in which the quote can be found. These citations are keyed to the Bibliography at the back of the workbook should you wish to read certain works more fully.

Throughout the workbook you will see this symbol   . When you come to the symbol, please stop. Do not read any further; think and reflect as you are requested to do in order to internalize the ideas being shared or the experience reflected upon.

Reflecting and Recording

After the reading each day, there will be a time for reflecting and recording. This dimension calls for you to record some of your reflections. The degree of meaning you receive from this workbook is largely dependent upon your faithfulness to its practice. You may be unable on a particular day to do precisely what is requested. If so, then simply record that fact and make a note of why you can't follow through. This may give you some insight about yourself and help you to grow.

Also, on some days there may be more suggestions than you can deal with in the time you have. Do what is most meaningful for you and do not feel guilty.

Finally, always remember that this is a personal pilgrimage. What you write in your workbook is your private property. You may not wish to share it with anyone. For this reason no two people should attempt to share the same workbook. The importance of what you write is not what it may mean to someone else but what it means to you. Writing, even if it is only brief notes or single-word reminders, helps us clarify our feelings and thinking.

The significance of the reflecting and recording dimension will grow as you move along. Even beyond the eight weeks, you will find meaning in looking back to what you wrote on a particular day in response to a particular situation.

Sharing with Others

In the history of Christian spirituality, the spiritual director or guide has been a significant person. To varying degrees, most of us have had spiritual directors—persons to whom we have turned for support and direction in our spiritual pilgrimage. There is a sense in which this workbook can be a spiritual guide, for you can use it as a private venture without participating in a group.

Its meaning will be enhanced, however, if you share the adventure with eight to twelve others (larger numbers tend to limit individual involvement). In this way, you will profit from the growing insights of others, and they will profit from yours. A guide for group sharing is included in the text at the end of each week.

If this is a group venture, all persons should begin their personal involvement with the workbook on the same day, so that when you come together to share as a group, all of you will have been dealing with the same material and will be at the same place in the text. It will be helpful if you have an initial get-acquainted group meeting to begin the adventure. A guide for this meeting is provided in this introduction.

Group sessions for this workbook are designed to last one and one-half hours (with the exception of the initial meeting). Those sharing in the group should covenant to attend all sessions unless an emergency prevents attendance. There will be eight weekly sessions in addition to this first get-acquainted time.

One person may provide the leadership for the entire eight weeks or leaders may be assigned from week to week. The leader's tasks are as follows:

1. Read the directions and determine ahead of time how to handle the session. It may not be possible to use all the suggestions for sharing and praying together. Feel free to select those you think will be most meaningful and those for which you have adequate time.

2. Model a style of openness, honesty, and warmth. A leader should not ask anyone to share what he or she is not willing to share. Usually, the leader should be the first to share, especially as it relates to personal experiences.

3. Moderate the discussion.

4. Encourage reluctant members to participate and try to prevent a few persons from doing all the talking.

5. Keep the sharing centered in personal experience rather than academic debate.

6. Honor the time schedule. If it appears necessary to go longer than one and one-half hours, the leader should get consensus for continuing another twenty or thirty minutes.

7. See that the meeting time and place are known by all, especially if meetings are held in different homes.

8. Make sure that the necessary materials for meetings are available and that the meeting room is arranged ahead of time.

It is a good idea for weekly meetings to be held in the homes of the participants. (Hosts or hostesses should make sure there are as few interruptions as possible from children, telephones, pets, and so forth.) If the meetings are held in a church, they should be in an informal setting. Participants are asked to dress casually, to be comfortable and relaxed.

If refreshments are served, they should come after the formal meeting. In this way, those who wish to stay longer for informal discussion may do so, while those who need to keep to the time schedule will be free to leave but will get the full value of the meeting time.

Suggestions for Initial Get-Acquainted Meeting

Since the initial meeting is for the purpose of getting acquainted and beginning the shared pilgrimage, here is a way to get started.

1.   Have each person in the group give his or her full name and the name by which each wishes to be called. Address all persons by the first name or nickname. If name tags are needed, provide them. Each person should make a list of the names somewhere in his or her workbook.

2.   Let each person in the group share one of the happiest, most exciting, or most meaningful experiences he or she has had during the past three or four weeks.

3.   After this experience of happy sharing, ask each person who will to share his or her expectations of this workbook study. Why did he or she become a part of it? What does each expect to gain from it? What are the reservations?

4.   The leader should now review the introduction to the workbook and ask if there are questions about directions and procedures. (The leader should have read the introduction prior to the meeting.) If persons have not received copies of the workbook, the books should be handed out now. Remember that every person must have his or her own workbook.

5.   Day One in the workbook is the day following this initial meeting, and the next meeting should be held on Day Seven of the first week. If the group must choose a weekly meeting time other than seven days from this initial session, the reading assignment should be adjusted so that the weekly meetings are always on Day Seven, and Day One is always the day following a weekly meeting.

6.   Nothing binds group members together more than praying for one another. The leader should encourage each participant to write the names of all persons in the group in his or her workbook and commit to praying for them by name daily during the eight weeks.

After checking to see that everyone knows the time and place of the next meeting, the leader should close with a prayer, thanking God for each person in the group and for the opportunity for growth.

Week One

Predicament
and Promise

Attracted to/Repelled by Goodness

Even though the desire to do good is in me, I am
not able to do it. I don't do the good I want to do;
instead, I do the evil that I do not want to do.
—Romans 7:18-19, TEV

From the dawn of time, we human beings have been both attracted to and repelled by the idea of goodness. We lift people up as heroes and saviors; yet relish the moment when they are exposed as having feet of clay. We spend countless dollars on books, videos, programs, and workshops hoping that they will help us "be all that we can be." Yet, we deliberately sabotage those very efforts with bad habits that have infiltrated our daily living. We want to be good, but we aren't always able. We don't completely like being bad, but we sometimes don't mind it. As Paul expressed, there seems to be a battle going on within us between the desire to follow the good and the allure of the evil that surrounds us. As I was contemplating this idea, I recalled a clapping game called "Miss Lucy" that I enjoyed playing as a child. There are endless variations to this game, and it seems to be somewhat timeless as my two girls now enjoy it immensely. Watching their enjoyment as they clap their hands together and sing the words illustrates the love-hate relationship we have with moral virtue. They sing:

> *Miss Lucy had a steamboat, the steamboat had a bell.*
> *Miss Lucy went to heaven, the steamboat went to helllll-o*
> *Operator, please dial me number nine.*
> *If you disconnect me, I'll kick you from behind . . .*
> *The frigerator, there was a piece of glass.*
> *Miss Lucy slipped and fell on it and broke her little assss-k*
> *Me no more questions, I'll tell you no more lies.*
> *The boys are in the bathroom, zipping up their flies . . .*
> *Are in the garden. The cows are in the shed.*
> *Miss Lucy and her boyfriend, are kissing in the bed!*

To witness the delight as my two little girls, ages five and eight, clap and sing is to recognize the battle taking place between the good and the evil within us. Their eyes light up mischievously as they draw out the forbidden words but then quickly add the ending that renders them harmless. Hellllllll-o operator! Asssssssssss-k me no more questions! The possibility of breaking the language rules of our household is enticing; yet, they don't really want to go all the way. Adults are no different. Vice is alluring, exciting; yet, we are not completely comfortable. The push and pull may even be so strong that there are times when we feel like two selves, one striving for the good, the other enjoying the bad.

This is the predicament of human kind. It is this predicament that Paul was referring to when he uttered his anguished cry, "Wretched man that I am! Who will rescue me from this body of death?" (Rom. 7:24). We are all torn between the good and the evil that surrounds us. Recognizing this conflict within us is not a call to wallow in guilt or shame over the sin that attracts us; nor is it an opportunity to throw up our hands in helpless resignation over the seeming impossibility of consistently doing good. It is simply the recognition of an objective fact. But it is an important recognition that must be made if we are to ever resolve this conflict.

A second step in addressing this struggle is to remember that as human beings, we all belong to a God who created each of us as one good, whole self. Granted, somewhere along the way something happened to that good, whole self. Our wholeness became marred by fragmentation and estrangement; and our goodness became supremely vulnerable and responsive to the presence of evil. Yet, our freedom to choose has never disappeared. We were not created to be puppets or robots. We like to put it this way: Each of us is a unique, unrepeatable miracle of God. God wants each of us to recognize that we belong to God. God desires our free choosing of relationship, just as God freely chose to create us in the first place. Because of this freedom, we do not have to succumb to our inner responsiveness to evil. We can remember that "God saw everything that he had made, and indeed, it was very good" (Gen. 1:31). We are always free to choose to be the good self God created us to be, or to become captivated by the evil that is all around us.

REFLECTING AND RECORDING

Spend four or five minutes, reflecting on the assertion that human beings are both attracted to and repelled by the idea of goodness. Have you found this to be true in the lives of your family, friends, and community? What about in your own life?

Recall your most recent experience of being torn between a good choice and an evil choice. Make some notes, naming the choices, describing some of your feelings and how you made your choices.

DURING THE DAY

Stay alert to the pull of good and evil in the choices you make today—be especially sensitive to the subtle differences.

DAY TWO

Grace as Resolution to Predicament

While we were still weak, at the right time Christ died for the ungodly. Indeed, rarely will anyone die for a righteous person—though perhaps for a good person someone might actually dare to die. But God proves his love for us in that while we still were sinners Christ died for us. Much more surely then, now that we have been justified by his blood, will we be saved through him from the wrath of God. For if while we were enemies, we were reconciled to God through the death of his Son, much more surely, having been reconciled, will we be saved by his life.

—Romans 5:6-10

Yesterday we began by pointing to the conflict experienced in our lives between good and evil. We emphasized that two steps in actively addressing this struggle are, first, an objective recognition of the conflict itself; and second, remembering that we all belong to God who created each of us as one good, whole self.

The next step on our journey is the realization that we do not have to fight this battle alone. We believe that God offers hope for us as we seek to find a resolution to our struggle. The foundation of that hope is Jesus Christ, who through his death and resurrection has conquered the power of evil in the world. "For this purpose the Son of God was manifested, that he might destroy the works of the devil" (1 John 3:8, KJV). The witness of scripture is clear: Evil is a conquered foe. Our hope is not just in hearing that message, but in actually experiencing that victory in our lives. We believe that in any given situation, God's grace is more powerful than the lure of temptation. As we seek to resolve the struggle within us, that is where we must begin—with God's grace.

God's grace comes in many ways, two of which are at the heart of the Christian faith and experience: justification and sanctification. These are theological words that point to two basic experiences in our lives. The first, justification, is the experience of becoming right with God. Justifying grace is the redemptive, healing, recreating love of God that comes to us as a gift. When we recognize our sinfulness, earnestly repent and accept the pardon that God offers us through Jesus Christ, justifying grace works in our lives to heal our relationship with God. The word *justification* means "to make right." Accepting God's gracious love and forgiveness, we are made right with God, reconciled, brought back into relationship with God.

While justification is something God does for us, sanctification is something God does *in* us. John Wesley used the metaphor of a house. The house is our lifetime relationship with God. The front door is justifying grace. By opening the door and accepting the gift of grace and pardon that God offers, we are justified; we're made right with God. Once we cross the threshold of the house through our experience of justification, we begin to experience sanctifying grace.

Sanctifying grace is the grace that remains with us and empowers us as we move throughout the house of life. As we live our lives, moving from room to room, God's grace is with us to strengthen us and give us the power to face whatever challenges we encounter within each room of our life and also to shape our lives after the likeness of Christ. Thus, while justification is the experience of an event, sanctification is a process, the life-long experience of spiritual growth, empowered by God's grace.

So, grace comes to us in two specific ways. One, as the undeserved favor of God for our justification. Though we are unworthy and undeserving, though separated from God because of our sin, God accepts us into a restored relationship with God. Two, God's grace comes as the power of the Holy Spirit, enabling us to live in the ways of God. Putting those two expressions together means that the grace of God not only justifies sinners, but also transforms and renews them.

As we enter the contest between good and evil, we are armed with the power of God's grace. This is a power that has already won the victory. It remains only for us to claim that victory in the everyday living of our lives.

REFLECTING AND RECORDING

Recall your experience of justification. We referred to this as an event. Don't be thrown off by that. Our total Christian experience is cumulative; it's a process. Grace comes at time in our lives when we claim our justification, own the fact that we are forgiven, accepted by God as we are, loved unconditionally. Reflect on your experience of justification. Make some notes about your experience. What went on in your life, your feelings, the action you took, the time frame, including the specific occasion when you claimed your justification?

Now write a paragraph about significant events, developments, experiences or relationships that you would identify with sanctification.

Spend a few minutes reflecting on the assertion that *evil is a conquered foe.*

DURING THE DAY

Sanctifying grace has no meaning apart from everyday life—our actions and attitudes. Look for occasions today when you need sanctifying grace; claim that power.

Virtues as Gifts of Power

God is able to make all grace abound to you, so that in all things at all times, having all that you need, you will abound in every good work. As it is written: "He has scattered abroad his gifts to the poor; his righteousness endures forever." Now he who supplies seed to the sower and bread for food will also supply and increase your store of seed and will enlarge the harvest of your righteousness.

—2 Corinthians 9:8-10, NIV

Justification and sanctification are two major aspects of God's grace; they are not the only manifestations of God's love for us. There is a sense in which the seven cardinal virtues—wisdom, courage, justice, temperance, faith, hope, and love—are expressions of sanctification, God's gifts of grace to us. As gifts of grace, they are indications of God's goodness in our lives. Because they are gifts of grace, they are also gifts of power. The Greek word *arete* is the word from which we get our word *virtue*; it literally means power. Therefore, the virtues are evidence of God's power of goodness at work within us.

By providing us with these gifts of power, God has given us a means by which we can address the conflict in which we find ourselves daily. As we explore these virtues in the coming weeks, we need to keep the idea of power firmly in our minds. The virtues are not simply moral skills that we attempt to master, they are a source of power in developing our character because they are God's gifts of grace to us. Therefore, as we seek to be the good selves God created us to be, we do not have to, in fact we cannot, depend on our own resources. Rather we have the power of God's grace to create, guide, and strengthen us.

In the book *Schindler's List*, Thomas Keneally tells the story of Oskar Schindler, whom he describes as a "German bon vivant, speculator, charmer, and sign of contradiction." Keneally goes to great lengths to emphasize that Schindler was anything but virtuous. A married man, he kept a German mistress while having another affair with his Polish secretary. He was a drinker. He initially profited from the German war effort and served as a prison camp director. Yet, Schindler's story is remarkable. Using his position as a German industrialist, and later as the overseer of a prison camp, he was able through shrewd and often underhanded means to save more Jews than any other single person during World War II. His story is moving and powerful; yet much of its power comes from the fact that Oskar Schindler was such an ordinary human being. He rose from obscurity before the war and returned to obscurity afterwards. His overall life was not one marked by virtue; yet for a few crucial years, he rose to the challenge before him, acting with courage and wisdom, working for justice, and motivated by love.

The virtue that Oskar Schindler exhibited during those difficult years is evidence of the power of God's grace to act in our lives. Left to our own devices, we continue along a mediocre path; attuned to the power of God's grace in our lives, we are provided the means to do great things.

REFLECTING AND RECORDING

Think about the idea that the virtues are God's gifts of grace to us that empower us for the moral life. Have you accepted that power for yourself? Do you find yourself depending on your own strength of character to lead you toward the moral life?

In three or four sentences, describe a failed effort on your part to exercise virtue or lead a moral life in your own power.

In three or four sentences, describe a situation when you acted morally in the face of temptation, empowered by a force not your own.

DURING THE DAY

Be mindful that while you have to make moral decisions, the power to act is not yours alone. Call upon God's grace.

DAY FOUR

Virtues Are Gifts of
Grace Offered to All People

We have emphasized that the virtues are a source of power for us, not simply a set of moral skills to be acquired. Their power lies in the fact that they are God-given, rather than humanly achieved. This can be a great source of confidence for us. We are not alone in our quest to be the good selves God created us to be! God desires for us to be whole and is available always to provide us with the power to become complete and full human beings.

Because the virtues are gracious gifts of God that show the power of God's goodness and love, they are offered to all people. Each of us, regardless of our background, has access to the power of these virtues. They are natural graces that are available to us simply because we are human; because God desires all human beings to be whole and is dedicated to empowering them to be so. Paul was referring to this when he wrote to the Romans:

> *It is not the hearers of the law who are righteous in God's sight, but the doers of the law who will be justified. When the Gentiles, who do not possess the law, do instinctively what the law requires, these, though not having the law are a law to themselves. They show that what the law requires is written on their hearts, to which their own conscience also bears witness; and their conflicting thoughts will accuse or perhaps excuse them on the day when, according to my gospel, God, through Jesus Christ, will judge the secret thoughts of all.*
>
> —Romans 2:13-16

From the Christian perspective, the Gentiles are the world. This is a significant point for us as we begin our study. One of the unfortunate side effects of sin is that it causes us to delude ourselves into thinking that we, and we alone, are standing on the moral high ground. Certainly there are times when we are blessed with insight and are indeed able to stand confidently on that hallowed hill. However, more times than not we are mistaken; and our mistake is all the more grievous because we believe that we and/or our group is alone in rightfully claiming the moral high ground. Our sin makes us unwilling to entertain the possibility that there might be a basis of legitimate, morally worthy opposition to ourselves. We can't bring ourselves to admit that the people who disagree with us may have come to their conclusions through deliberate, thoughtful, maybe even prayerful, consideration. This is hard for us to do because it makes us aware of the possibility that we might be wrong and need to change our minds. It's much easier and more comfortable to believe that the other person is either crazy or stupid, or just not thinking straight. It makes us feel better about ourselves and our opinions, when we convince ourselves that if people just listened to us and tried to understand our point of view, they would change their minds and agree with us.

Paul's assertion makes it clear that true moral character is not a matter of simply belonging to a particular group, or holding a particular viewpoint. God provides all people, Christians and others, with the gracious power of the virtues. God offers them to everyone as a means of moving toward the good selves God created us to be. This means that if we are to take the virtues seriously in our own lives, we must also take them seriously in the lives of others. We must recognize that there may be others who disagree with us or who appear different from us, but who are also seeking to be morally serious in their lives. At the very least, this kind of recognition can open us to the opportunity for dialogue and productivity rather than accusation and acrimony. At its best, it can open us to the possibility of widening the commitment to the moral life that our society so badly needs.

The challenging implication is that God provides all people, at least potentially, with the gracious power of the virtues. When we encounter others who think differently than we do, our wish should not be that they think like we do, but that they think like God does. That should be our prayer for ourselves, to think like God.

REFLECTING AND RECORDING

Spend some time in self-examination, bringing your mindset and attitudes into the light of these questions:

(1) Do I give other people the benefit of the doubt—accepting the possibility that they are morally serious, and may be more right than I am?

(2) Am I willing to put my moral judgments alongside those of others to be evaluated in the marketplace of the pursuit of a moral order?

List two or three issues that you have strong convictions about.

Beside each of the issues, write the names of persons or groups which you know disagree with you.

Are you willing to listen and learn from those you have listed? Are you willing to give them the benefit of the doubt? Spend a few minutes reflecting on these questions.

DURING THE DAY

As you go through the day and encounter persons who think differently than you, pray for them—not that they think like you, but that they think like God.

DAY FIVE

Virtues Are Habits

[God] will repay according to each one's deeds: to those who by patiently doing good seek for glory and honor and immortality, he will give eternal life; while for those who are self-seeking and who obey not the truth but wickedness, there will be wrath and fury
—Romans 2:6-8

Thomas Aquinas was one of the great champions of developing the virtues in our moral life. He described the two sides of virtue: power and habit. During the last several days we explored the aspect of power; now we turn to the idea of habit.

A habit is the fruit of repetition. The more we repeat a certain act, the more it becomes ingrained in us to do it; so that eventually, we do it without even thinking about it. Human beings are creatures of habit. If you don't believe this, take note of your morning and nighttime preparations. Do you do the same things or is each time different? How do you put your clothes on each morning? Do you put the same leg into your pants first every time?

My husband and son are wonderful case studies of habits. My husband, John, has an apple and a cup of coffee each morning before work, rain or shine. During the week, unless there's something special going on, he eats a turkey sandwich for lunch and has done so for as long as I can remember. Not surprisingly, my son takes after his father. It is crucial that Nathan wake up at 7:00 AM each school day. He doesn't need to leave for school until 8:00 and it only takes him about fifteen minutes to eat and get dressed, but if he oversleeps, it's not a good thing. Similarly, he has a bowl of ice cream *every night* before he goes to bed—every night. Recently he needed some help with a knotted soccer cleat, and when John began to help him get it on he said, "I don't like putting this shoe on first. Do the other one first."

Predictability, routine. We may chuckle at our idiosyncrasies, but our habits can provide us with a sense of security and stability. When they are healthy and not compulsive, our habits can help to bring order and efficiency to our lives. Like all habits, good and bad, virtues develop through repetition and exercise. While God's power in the virtues is essential, it will not be effective in our lives unless we are able to channel that power through disciplined practice. Moral development is much like a runner in training. God may have blessed the runner with the talent and power to run, but he or she will not be able to compete successfully without hours of dedicated and rigorous practice.

Our use of the virtues is the same. We have the power from God, but we will not be successful unless we devote ourselves to diligent rehearsal. Developing our moral selves, then, is a day-by-day, step-by-step process of determination. It often involves making hard choices and following "the road less traveled." In order to strengthen our characters, and move toward the good selves God created us to be, we need both the power of God's grace in the virtues, and our own disciplined exercise of them. When this combination is experienced, we encounter the possibility of the habits of virtue becoming second nature, thus perfecting our created nature.

REFLECTING AND RECORDING

Think about your daily routine. Are you a creature of habit? Make a list of some of your daily habits.

Now look at each habit on your list. Is it healthy or compulsive, maybe unhealthy?

Now think about a challenge that you have faced recently. Did it involve commitment to practice and training? Were you inclined toward diligence?

Contemplate your commitment to exploring the virtues. Are you willing to dedicate yourself to the effort that may be required? How might this dedication necessitate a change in other habits?

DURING THE DAY

Pay attention to all the things you do today by habit. Especially be attentive to the good and positive things you do without question, actions and responses that are second nature because of habit.

DAY SIX

Why Should We Strive for Goodness?

We began our study with the exploration of the human predicament and our means of resolving that conflict; yet, some may still be wondering why we should strive for resolution at all. Is it so bad muddling along as we always have? We believe that the issue is not that the status quo is so horrible, though for some it truly is. The issue is falling so short of what God created us to be. We believe the moral life is worth striving for because it is for this that God created us. Paul tells us in Ephesians 2:10, "We are what he has made us, created in Christ Jesus for good works, which God prepared beforehand to be our way of life." The word Paul uses when he says that we are what he has made us, is the Greek word *poiema*, which can be translated "work of art." We are God's work of art and we were made for goodness. When we fall short of that calling, we become strangers both to ourselves and to God. However, when we accept God's gift of power and work toward the goal of becoming the good selves God created us to be, we find happiness. This is not a surface, psychological happiness, or simply feeling good. Rather, it is a deeply rooted sense of doing what we were created to do and being the type of person we were created to be.

Jesus alluded to this type of deep happiness when he talked about "blessedness" in the Sermon on the Mount.

> *Blessed are the poor in spirit, for theirs is the kingdom of heaven.*
> *Blessed are those who mourn, for they will be comforted. Blessed*
> *are the meek, for they will inherit the earth. Blessed are those*
> *who hunger and thirst for righteousness, for they will be filled.*
> *Blessed are the merciful, for they shall receive mercy. Blessed are*

the pure in heart, for they will see God. Blessed are the peace-makers, for they will be called children of God.

—Matthew 5:3-9

It is this kind of deep happiness, this kind of blessedness, that comes when we are able to live in the joy of God's presence and in the loving community of God's people.

In the movie *Chariots of Fire*, a young Scottish missionary delays his plan to go to China in order to run in the Olympics. His sister tries to convince him to stop running and focus again on his mission work. His reply points to the deep happiness we're speaking about: "I believe God made me for a purpose: that's China. But he also made me fast, and when I run I feel His pleasure." When we live according to our purpose, when we choose to be the good self God created us to be, we will experience true happiness; we will feel God's pleasure.

REFLECTING AND RECORDING

What is the one thing you do which makes you feel most God's pleasure?

Write a prayer expressing thanksgiving to God for creating you as a work of art, and confessing your failure to be what God created you to be.

DURING THE DAY

Pay close attention to people today, taking note of which ones seem to feel God's pleasure in what they are doing.

DAY SEVEN

How We Begin

Throughout this week we have focused in a general way on the challenge of striving to be the good self God created us to be. We lifted up the importance of recognizing the basic human predicament of being both attracted to and repelled by goodness; and we emphasized our need to remember that we were created by a loving God who desires our relationship and wholeness. We stressed that God's grace is the means of our power in resolving the inner conflict between good and evil; and asserted that the virtues themselves are God's gifts of grace for power, offered to all people. We affirmed that the virtues are also habits which are formed within us through the power of God's grace as well as through our disciplined training and practice. We maintained that the moral life is worth pursuing with such discipline because it moves us closer to our created purpose, goodness; and creates within us the kind of true happiness that comes with being what we were meant to be.

With all of that in mind, there remains the practical question of where we begin if we are seeking to strengthen our moral lives. At the most basic level, we each must begin with moral sincerity. We must truly *want* to be good. For some, that might mean asking God to *help us* want to be good. At another level, we must start where we are. We must ask for and accept the forgiveness God offers so that we can be free from guilt over our past. For some this is not a new element of our faith, but an ongoing part of our spiritual journey. For others this may be a giant first step, an integral part of our complete conversion experience. If that is the case, we may be encountering an entirely new way of thinking, feeling, seeing, and, of course, behaving. For all of us, however, it is Christ who offers the power to undergo that transformation.

The transformation of our moral selves does not occur in a vacuum, however. We believe that virtue can and should be taught:

> *Hear, O Israel: The Lord is our God, the Lord alone. You shall love the Lord your God with all your heart, and with all your soul, and with all your might. Keep these words that I am commanding you today in your heart. Recite them to your children and talk about them when you are at home and when you are away, when you lie down and when you rise. Bind them as a sign on your hand, fix them as an emblem on your forehead, and write them on the doorposts of your house and on your gates.*
>
> —Deuteronomy 6:4-9

Yet virtue cannot be taught unless it is a "lived reality" within the community of faith. We are social beings who are shaped by the communities that surround us. Another practical beginning point, then, is the recognition that virtue is nurtured through purposeful communities that treasure goodness and whose vocation is to teach and live the moral life. While this workbook may be helpful on a personal level, our striving for the moral life will not be consistently fruitful without the support of a morally serious community that can provide reinforcement and guidance.

As you begin to explore the virtues in more detail, recognize that serious study does not imply any claim to perfection. It simply acknowledges that we see the goal; we know what we want to be, and we know the importance of it.

One final word: Simplicity and a sense of humor are always assets to any spiritual endeavor. If you know something is wrong, simply don't do it; and in all things remember that virtue is much too serious an endeavor to be solemn. An ability to laugh at our mistakes and foibles will lighten our load as we journey through the moral life.

REFLECTING AND RECORDING

Examine where you are in your quest for virtue by reflecting on the following. Spend some time thinking about each question:

1. In what ways do you genuinely want to be good?
2. How are you seeking moral sincerity and integrity?
3. Are you in regular fellowship with persons who are committed to the moral life?
4. Identify relationships with persons whom you would consider mentors in the virtuous life?

DURING THE DAY

Take this word as a guide for your life today: *If something is wrong, simply don't do it.*

If you are a part of a group using this workbook, this should be your meeting day. Call two or three persons in the group, telling them how happy you are to be sharing this venture with them.

GROUP MEETING FOR WEEK ONE

Introduction

These group sessions will be most meaningful as they reflect the experience of all the participants. This guide is simply an effort to facilitate personal sharing. Therefore, do not be rigid in following these suggestions. The leader, especially, should seek to be sensitive to what's going on in the lives of the participants and to focus the group's sharing of those experiences. Ideas are important. We should wrestle with new ideas as well as with ideas with which we disagree It is important, however, that the group meeting not become a debate about ideas. The emphasis should be on persons—experiences, feelings, and meaning. Content is important—but how content applies to our individual lives, our relationship to God and others, is most important.

As the group comes to the place where all can share honestly and openly what is happening in their lives, the more meaningful the experience will be. This does not mean sharing only the good or positive; share also the struggles, the difficulties, the negatives.

This process is not easy; it is deceptive to pretend it is. Growth requires effort. Don't be afraid to share your questions, reservations, and "dry periods," as well as that in which you find meaning.

Sharing Together

1. Take five to ten minutes and talk generally about your experience with the workbook. What difficulties are you encountering? What are you finding most meaningful?

2. Invite one or two persons to share their most recent experience of being torn between a good choice and an evil choice.

3. Now talk for four or five minutes to reflect on the assertion that persons are both attracted to and repelled by goodness.

4. Invite two or three persons to share their experience of "justification."

5. Spend five to eight minutes discussing "sanctification." As you talk, be sure to share personal experiences, developments or relationships that have contributed to your sanctification.

6. Spend ten to twelve minutes talking about virtue. Explore the notions that virtues are God's gifts to empower us for the moral life and that virtues are God's gifts offered to all people. How do these notions harmonize with the idea that virtue must be cultivated?

7. Invite as many persons as will to share one thing they do which makes them feel God's pleasure. (See Reflecting and Recording, Day Six, page 26)

8. Close your sharing time by discussing your responses to the questions in the Reflecting and Recording period of Day Seven, page 28.

Praying Together

Each week the group is asked to pray together. Corporate prayer is one of the great blessings of Christian community. There is a power in corporate prayer, and it is important that this dimension be included in our shared pilgrimage.

It is also important that you feel comfortable in this and that no pressure be placed on anyone to pray aloud. God does not need to hear our words spoken aloud to hear our prayers. Silence, where thinking is centered and attention is focused, may provide our deepest periods of prayer.

Verbal prayers should be offered spontaneously as a person chooses to pray aloud—not "let's go around the circle now, and each one pray."

Suggestions for this "praying together" time will be given each week. The leader for the week should regard these only as suggestions. What is happening in the meeting—the mood, the needs that are expressed, the timing-should determine the direction for the group praying together. There may be occasions when in the midst of your "sharing together" you will want to simply stop and offer prayer. Here are some possibilities for this closing period.

1.   Let the group think back over the sharing that has taken place during this session. What personal needs or concerns came out of the sharing? Begin to speak these aloud—any person verbalizing a need or a concern that has been expressed. Don't hesitate to mention a concern that you may have picked up from another, for example, "Mary isn't able to be with us this week because her son is in the hospital. Let's pray for her son and for her."

It will be helpful for each person to make notes of the concerns and needs that are mentioned. Enter deliberately into a period of silence. Let the leader verbalize each of these needs successively, allowing for a brief period following each so that persons in the group may center their attention and focus their prayers on the person, need, or concern mentioned. All of this will be in silence as each person prays in his or her own way.

2.   Invite any two persons to offer a spontaneous brief verbal prayer: 1) Thank God for the group and the opportunity to share with others in this study/learning/prayer experience. 2) Confess that we are all sinners in need of God's love and forgiveness, and ask God to open each of us to ourselves and to one another, to be honest in our sharing and genuinely caring for one another, and to be open to receive truth as it comes from God.

3.   Invite two people to read the prayers they wrote during their Reflecting and Recording on Day 6, page 26.

4.   If someone has an instant-developing camera, take a picture of each person in the group. Turn pictures facedown on the table and let each person take one. This is the person for whom you will pray specifically this week. Before you go, take a few minutes to visit with the person whose picture you chose, getting to know him/her better. Ask if there are things coming up in that person's life about which you might pray. If an instant camera is not available, write the name of each person in your group on a slip of paper and have each person draw a name.

Week Two

Wisdom and Courage

Trees "Which Yield Their Fruit"

Many years ago my father planted six pecan trees on his little farm. I don't know what happened. I know he planted them too close together and my hunch is he never fertilized them. Every time I visit my father I am disappointed with those trees. They have never fulfilled their purpose. They remain barren to this day.

The Bible is full of stories about trees and fruit. Jesus told a parable about a barren fig tree which the master of the vineyard would have cut down had the gardener not convinced him to give him time to work with it, fertilize and cultivate it for one more year (Luke 13:6-9). Then if it did not bear fruit he would cut it down. In one of Jesus' most challenging teachings he used the metaphor of trees and fruit. "No good tree bears bad fruit, nor again does a bad tree bear good fruit; for each tree is known by its own fruit. Figs are not gathered from thorns, nor are grapes picked from a bramble bush" (Luke 6:43-44). One of Jesus' harshest acts came one day when he was hungry and sought fruit from a fig tree. Finding nothing but leaves when it should have had figs, Jesus cursed it: "May no fruit ever come from you again!" (Matt. 21:19).

The very first psalm provides a challenging metaphor: trees which yield their fruit.

> *Happy are those who do not follow the advice of the wicked, or take the path that sinners tread, or sit in the seat of scoffers; but their delight is in the law of the LORD, and on his law they meditate day and night. They are like trees planted by streams of water, which yield their fruit in its season, and their leaves do not wither. In all that they do, they prosper. The wicked are not so, but are like the chaff that the wind drives away. Therefore the wicked will not stand in the judgment, nor sinners in the congregation of the righteous; for the LORD watches over the way of the righteous, but the way of the wicked will perish.*
>
> —Psalm 1

The psalmist presents a graphic parallel. The godly person is like a tree planted by the water, which produces fruit in its season. The picture of the wicked, the "ungodly," is in stark contrast. The writer changes the metaphor. They "are like chaff that the wind drives away."

The prophet Jeremiah paints a similar contrast.

> *Thus says the LORD: Cursed are those who trust in mere mortals and make mere flesh their strength, whose hearts turn away from*

the LORD. They shall be like a shrub in the desert and shall not see when relief comes. They shall live in the parched places of the wilderness, in an uninhabited salt land. Blessed are those who trust in the LORD, whose trust is the LORD. They shall be like a tree planted by water, sending out its roots by the stream. It shall not fear when heat comes, and its leaves shall stay green; in the year of drought it is not anxious, and it does not cease to bear fruit.
—Jeremiah 17:5-8

The message is clear in both the psalm and the prophet. There are two choices: trust in ourselves or trust in God. Those who trust in themselves will be like chaff that "the wind drives away," "like a shrub in the desert." But the persons who trust in God are like "trees planted by streams of water which yield their fruit."

This workbook is about the cardinal and theological virtues, defined by the Church as wisdom, courage, justice, temperance, faith, hope, and love. It is also about the "fruits of the Spirit," named by the Apostle Paul in Galatians 5:22-23: love, joy, peace, patience, kindness, generosity, faithfulness, gentleness, and self-control. We will consider the virtues first, but in considering them, we want to keep the image of fruit alive in our minds. As we pursue a life of goodness, as Christians, we are pursuing a life of faith in God, and our "delight is in the law of the Lord." Trusting in God, as in Jeremiah's image, we shall be like trees planted by water. No matter what happens—how much "heat" comes, or whether "drought" pervades our lifescape—we are not anxious and we do not cease to bear fruit.

The classic virtues at which we look for the next two weeks are disciplines we exercise and ideals that we seek in our quest for goodness, for the life to which God calls. They are also the fruit that grows as our lives become as trees with roots going down deep into God's grace.

REFLECTING AND RECORDING

Name two persons who come to your mind as you ponder the image of "a tree planted by streams of water."

Describe those persons here. What are their character traits? How do they relate to persons? How do they reflect integrity and genuine goodness? How do they earnestly seek to be good?

Spend the balance of your time thinking about virtues as disciplines we exercise in our quest for goodness, and fruit that grows in our lives as we trust God.

DURING THE DAY

It is not easy to distinguish between virtue as a discipline being exercised or a fruit growing in one's life. Virtue as a discipline involves intentionality; fruit is expressed spontaneously. As you observe people today, take note of whether the virtue you see in them is a discipline they are exercising or a fruit that is growing in them.

DAY TWO

The Foundation of Virtue

Does not wisdom call, and does not understanding raise her voice? On the heights, beside the way, at the crossroads she takes her stand; beside the gates in front of the town, at the entrance of the portals she cries out: "To you, O people, I call, and my cry is to all that live. O simple ones, learn prudence; acquire intelligence, you who lack it. Hear, for I will speak noble things, and from my lips will come what is right; for my mouth will utter truth. . . . I, wisdom, live with prudence, and I attain knowledge and discretion. . . . I have good advice and sound wisdom; I have insight, I have strength. . . . The LORD created me at the beginning of his work, the first of his acts long ago."

—Proverbs 8:1-7, 12, 14, 22

Wisdom has always been the first of the virtues. It holds this distinctive position in part because it grounds all the other virtues. As we will see throughout this study, the virtues are interconnected, each adding and enhancing the value of the others; each needing the others to make it what it is. Yet, while the rest of the virtues work together to deepen the individual meaning of each, wisdom appears to provide a foundation for all of them. Wisdom is the stage upon which the roles of the other virtues are played out. Justice is crucial, but we are lost as to how to achieve it without wisdom to guide us when interests compete. Courage is laudable, but it is mere rashness without wisdom to steer it toward a moral cause. Patience is important, but it becomes sabotage without wisdom to help us discern when the time for response is upon us. Love is the more excellent way, but it becomes simple sentiment without wisdom to shepherd us as we seek to put it into action.

When we speak of the virtues, we are speaking of the mystery of goodness. There is much we will never be able to comprehend or achieve. Wisdom, however, is the search for the truth in the midst of that mystery. For the Greek philosophers wisdom was the intellectual virtue of knowing the truth. There are two blocks to truth: ignorance and ideology. Ignorance is simply not knowing; it is not having wisdom because we do not know the truth. In contrast, ideology is the twisting of the truth for the purpose of power; we do not have wisdom because we have altered the truth for our own purposes.

In the biblical sense, there is more to wisdom than simply having knowledge. Thus, while ignorance was a great enemy in Greek philosophy, from the biblical perspective ideology is the far greater evil. In the Christian sense, you can be wise without a great deal of knowledge; but you will never have wisdom if you seek to twist the truth. Rather than being an intellectual virtue, biblical wisdom contains a distinctly moral component. That component is prudence. We can have intellectual virtue but without the moral component of prudence we will not have wisdom.

Wisdom as prudence is a form of practical and moral reasoning. It is the art of taking the time necessary to think things through and anticipate what might happen. It is the common sense virtue of discerning what is true, what is right, and how to live. During the course of these next several weeks, we will discover how badly we need, as individuals and as a society, to awaken the virtues. As we seek to awaken them we must first begin with wisdom. We no longer live in a world where order prevails; where there is one prevailing way and one prevailing truth. We live in a world of chaos, of diversity and competing truths. It is in this world that we must rediscover wisdom and in so doing approach the mystery of goodness and draw closer to God.

REFLECTING AND RECORDING

What sort of conflicts exist in your community—warring forces, each claiming to have the truth? List some of them.

Spend a few minutes thinking about how these forces may be twisting the truth for the purpose of power.

Within the Christian community, local and national, do you see signs of "competing truth" that threaten the unity of the Body of Christ? Name them.

Spend the balance of your time considering this claim: Ideology is the twisting of the truth for the purpose of power; we do not have wisdom because we have altered the truth for our own purposes.

DURING THE DAY

As you read the newspaper and watch television news for the next few days, look for situations where ignorance and ideology are blocks to truth and wisdom.

DAY THREE

Greater Than Knowledge

Trust in the Lord *with all your heart, and do not rely on your own insight. In all your ways acknowledge him, and he will make straight your paths.*

—Proverbs 3:5-6

One of the great myths of the modern era is that humanity can experience perpetual, boundless progress through the application of scientific reasoning. If we look back at events of the twentieth century, it is easy to see how this myth took shape. Electricity, the telephone, automobiles, airplanes, smallpox and polio vaccines, organ transplants, computers, all turned the world into a place where anything seemed possible. Unfortunately, the inadvertent side effect of the remarkable achievements of this century was the capacity to kill unimaginable numbers of people. As the world became smaller, people were confronted with other perspectives, and cultures began to clash. Only in this century has the struggle between ideas and convictions been backed up by such advanced weapons as the tank, bomber aircraft, and even nuclear weapons. Countless numbers of people, civilian and military, have been lost in battles of belief.

With all this progress, with all the new technology that seems to be appearing every day, we have not been able to produce a better human being. The myth of limitless progress may be perpetuated by science's ability to make people better on the outside, but there has been no improvement on the inside. Human beings are still plagued by the age-old problems of hate, anger, jealousy, greed, and a hunger for power.

In this, the post-modern era, the collapse of the modern myth of progress has some very compelling lessons to teach us. For our purposes today, the foremost is that knowledge isn't enough. We may be able to probe the surface of Mars, to place unfathomable amounts of information on a computer chip smaller than the size of your fingernail, to bring life to the dying through organ transplantation, but we seem unable to bring justice to the oppressed, reconciliation to the estranged, hope to the brokenhearted.

Wisdom begins where knowledge ends. We've heard that wisdom is our intelligence plus God's love, presence, and purpose. Proverbs says that reverence for the Lord is the beginning of wisdom (Prov. 9:10). True wisdom begins when we recognize the limits of our own human wisdom, when we perceive our need for the sustaining power of God in our lives. It begins when we turn to God in reverence. It flowers when we follow God in obedience.

The mother of a woman in a church I served was diagnosed with ovarian cancer. It was a serious diagnosis and she began treatment immediately. Not too long after treatment began, the woman herself was diagnosed with the same cancer. She began her treatment, and her mother continued in hers. Then a remarkable thing took place. The mother, in an act of complete self-giving, determined that she would forego the remainder of her treatment in order to be available to nurture and support her daughter, son-in-law, and three grandchildren through their medical crisis. This was a decision that, when viewed through the lens of knowledge alone, made no sense. We all know there is no guarantee in the treatment of cancer. With treatment we may have a chance, but without it we face certain death. Knowledge alone cannot explain such a choice. Yet this determination was certainly guided by wisdom. No other course so fully embodied the self-emptying love of Jesus Christ. No other course so completely personified the love God feels for each of us. The woman survived her battle with cancer; her mother did not. But the legacy of love, rooted in the wisdom of a courageous choice, lives on.

Wisdom needs knowledge, yes; but wisdom surpasses knowledge. When we open ourselves to God's direction in our lives, when we follow the urgings God plants in our hearts, when we utilize our knowledge for the sake of love, we come close to living a life of wisdom. That wisdom can then guide us and strengthen us as we seek to incorporate the other virtues into our lives as well.

REFLECTING AND RECORDING

Recall and describe an experience of wisdom that transcended "human thinking" and knowledge.

Looking back on the past two or three years, locate occasions and relationships when you were given a wisdom not your own. Describe those.

DURING THE DAY

As you observe people, watch television, and read the newspaper during the coming days, seek to identify stories of people acting not out of knowledge and human understanding but with a wisdom beyond themselves.

DAY FOUR

Spiritual Health: The Goal of Wisdom

How terrible for the world that there are things that make people lose their faith! Such things will always happen—but how terrible for the one who causes them! If your hand or your foot makes you lose your faith, cut it off and throw it away! It is better for you to enter life without a hand or a foot than to keep both hands and both feet and be thrown into the eternal fire.
—Matthew 18:7-8, TEV

Yesterday we explored the modern myth that knowledge and wisdom are the same thing. As Christians, we realize that this is not true; rather, we assert that wisdom includes, but also surpasses, knowledge. Wisdom is knowledge coupled with God's love, presence, and purpose. As we conclude our focus on wisdom, there is another myth that is important for us to explore; the myth that wisdom and knowledge are valuable for their own sake. From the biblical perspective this is patently false. Wisdom, as important as it is in and of itself and as crucial as it is to the foundation of all the other virtues, is not an end of its own. The end toward which wisdom—and all the virtues—points is relationship with God and spiritual wholeness and health. Wisdom is the means through which we gain a greater sense of personal wholeness and a restored relationship with our creator. It is the means through which we redirect ourselves toward our created purpose, goodness.

Jesus was keenly aware of the role of wisdom in regaining our spiritual health. One of the crucial aspects of his message and ministry was to urge people to get smart about their spiritual health. "If your right eye causes you to sin, take it out and throw it away!" (Matt. 5:29, TEV). If you are going to take the moral life seriously, make sure to surround yourself with good influences; if you value your safety, don't run with a dangerous crowd. Paul echoed Jesus' sentiment when he wrote to the Galatians 6:7, "Do not be deceived; God is not mocked, for you reap whatever you sow." We must be wise about our spiritual health. We must act in ways that protect, not endanger, our moral lives.

The Bible is one of the main tools available for us as we seek to use wisdom to bolster our spiritual health. Thomas Hobbes used the metaphor of a hedge fence to illustrate this. He talked about a highway on both sides of which the King had placed hedges. These hedges were not meant to stop travelers as they journeyed, but to keep them safely on the path. Jumping the hedge in order to take a short cut was always a possibility, but if you chose to leave the highway, you traveled at your own risk, taking the hazardous chance of traversing open country, without the aid of maps, and gambling with the possibility of encountering unforeseen dangers.

The Bible is our hedge as we travel on our spiritual journey. There are many places where the hedge is quite clear: the Ten Commandments, the Sermon on the Mount, the moral teaching throughout the entire book. We can always jump the hedge. But we do so at our own peril because then we enter open country, where there are no maps and many risks. Granted, there are many places where discerning the hedge is difficult because it is sparse or indistinct. God's Word is not always clear, particularly as we attempt to apply it with integrity to our post-modern world. It is easy to enter uncharted or poorly mapped moral territory. Yet, the existence of moral ambiguity should not be used as an excuse to jump over the clearly marked and well-defined hedges. Wisdom recognizes that there are moral principles that are always right, and breaking them is always wrong.

Wisdom is badly needed in our world today. History has shown that when we rationalize our jumping of the hedges of morality, destruction awaits. Unfortunately, we are destroying the hedges and have made loopholes in God's word. We have focused on right motive rather than on right behavior, on the love that is "in the heart" rather than on the love that has been shown to the neighbor. We have allowed the ends too often to justify the means; but, unfortunately, no one can accurately calculate all the consequences of our deeds. Wisdom understands that we need more than motives and consequences to guide us; we need hedges and a willingness to follow them.

Reverence for God is the beginning of wisdom. When we move from feeling that we ought to obey God to actually wanting to obey God, we have begun to cultivate wisdom and will begin to see the hedges that will foster our spiritual and moral growth and well-being.

Jesus' parable about the two men who built houses sums up well our discussion of wisdom (Matt. 7:24-27). There were two men who each built a house. The wise man built his house on rock, but the foolish man built his on the sand. Eventually, storms came and destroyed the house on the sand, but the house built on rock withstood the wind and rain. Jesus tells us that the wise man, the one who built his house on the rocks, is the one who hears and obeys God's word; and the foolish man is the one who hears, but does not obey. Wisdom guides us to build our houses on solid ground, the ground of faith with guidance from God. We must seek that wisdom. Our lives depend upon it.

REFLECTING AND RECORDING

Spend a bit of time thinking about the "hedge" as a metaphor for the guidance we have.

What things or persons or experiences make up the "hedges" which mark and keep you on your life-path? List those here.

Reflect for a moment on this statement: *Wisdom recognizes that there are moral principles that are always right, and breaking them is always wrong.*

List those moral principles you think are always right.

Think back on your own experience with these moral principles. Identify occasions in your own life when you have proven that breaking these principles is always wrong.

Name at least two areas in our society today where we have leaped over the hedge.

Spend a few minutes in prayer. Pray for the restoration of "hedges," the recovery of moral principles in our society. Examine your own life, and make whatever confession, repentance and commitment you need to make in relation to your need for wisdom and moral certainty.

DURING THE DAY

Observe occasions among persons and in the corporate life of society where we allow the ends to justify the means, where we excuse ourselves by having right motives, rather than demanding right behavior.

DAY FIVE

Courage—Strength of Heart

What then shall we say to these things? If God is for us, who can be against us? He who did not spare His own Son, but delivered Him up for us all, how shall He not with Him also freely give us

*all things? Who shall bring a charge against God's elect? It is God
who justifies. Who is he who condemns? It is Christ who died,
and furthermore is also risen, who is even at the right hand of
God, who also makes intercession for us. Who shall separate us
from the love of Christ? Shall tribulation, or distress, or persecution, or famine, or nakedness, or peril, or sword? As it is written:
"For Your sake we are killed all day long: We are accounted as
sheep for the slaughter." Yet in all these things we are more than
conquerors through Him who loved us. For I am persuaded that
neither death nor life, nor angels nor principalities nor powers,
nor things present nor things to come, nor height nor depth, nor
any other created thing, shall be able to separate us from the love
of God which is in Christ Jesus our Lord.*

—Romans 8:31-39, NKJV

Courage is one of the few virtues that has never gone out of style. It has always
been and probably always will be laudable in the eyes of both secular society and
the community of faith to have courage. The Greek word for courage, *andrea*, literally means "manliness." In Latin, the word is *fortitudo*, literally meaning physical
strength. That is where we get our physical and heroic ideas about courage. This
connotation of courage has been reinforced by the fact that both the Greek and
Latin words for courage have always had military overtones. For instance, courage
for Plato was the virtue particular to the soldier. It is interesting, however, that in
the entire New Testament, the Greek word for courage is never used. Instead,
when speaking about courage, the Bible uses words that relate to the heart:
strength of heart, boldness of speech, endurance of faith and hope.

To be sure, there is a physical element to courage. It is a natural evidence of
grace that some even call a biological grace. It is evidenced every time a woman
undertakes the physical rigors of pregnancy and risks her life during the trials of
childbirth. It is seen in firefighters and police officers and emergency medical per-
sonnel as they respond without hesitation to the needs of others. It is seen in
every "good Samaritan" who stops to render aid. It happens often without a great
deal of thought when our bodies seem to react more from adrenaline than from
any amount of intellectual decision-making. The saying that courage is "fear that
has said its prayers" hits the mark.

The physical element of courage provides a foundation for its meaning in that
in its most basic sense, courage is the ability to withstand fear or the threat of pain
or death. However, courage is not limited to the purely physical; there is a moral
element as well. The fear that we face in our lives does not always stem from the
physical arena, nor does the pain. Thus courage is needed in all areas of our lives:
physical, mental, emotional, moral, spiritual. Some have even said that courage is
the necessary ingredient for all the other virtues. We cannot be just in today's
world of injustice and oppression without courage. We cannot live temperately in
today's world of extremes without courage. We cannot love in today's world of
hate without courage. Yet, for courage to be courage, it cannot stand alone; it

needs the other virtues. There is a large difference between courage that faces danger for a just, wise and good reason and "guts" that faces danger for any reason at all. Courage needs the other virtues to keep it a true virtue; for there is no virtue in courage done for a valueless or malicious cause.

Biblical courage incorporates the physical and moves beyond it to relate to the heart. In so doing courage connects intimately with faith and hope. Courage is action rooted in the conviction that we are not alone. It is the fruit of life grounded in a trusting heart. Paul spoke of this grounding in trust when he asked, "Who will separate us from the love of Christ? Will hardship, or distress, or persecution, or famine, or nakedness, or peril, or sword?" (Rom. 8:35). He connects faith and courage again with his answer: not one thing! no one! nothing! "For I am convinced that neither death, nor life, nor angels, nor rulers, nor things present, nor things to come, nor powers, nor height, nor depth, nor anything else in all creation, will be able to separate us from the love of God in Christ Jesus our Lord." (Rom. 8:38-39). Biblical courage, Christian courage, is to live with the knowledge that we are not alone. As W. Paul Jones put it, courage is

> *. . . a heart confident that in Christ, God so enters the struggle of life with death that the ongoing Divine/human crucifixion can be lived under the hope of resurrection. Christian courage is the heart of faith experienced as trust.*
>
> —Jones, p. 13

Courage is faith that rests on "the assurance of things hoped for, the conviction of things not seen" (Heb. 11:1). Through our faith, God empowers us with a bold heart, which is courage expressed in daily living.

REFLECTING AND RECORDING

Look again at those persons you named on Day One of this week as you pondered on the image of "a tree planted by streams of water." Would you say they are persons of courage?

Spend a bit of time considering the suggestion that courage is the fruit—the action expression—of a trusting and bold heart.

Christian courage is to live with the knowledge that we are not alone. Can you think of a time in your life when you did not have the courage to do something you felt you should do? Make some notes describing that experience.

Looking back on this remembered experience, would you have acted differently if you had been absolutely confident that you were not alone—God was with you?

DURING THE DAY

Look for expressions of two kinds of courage today: 1) *andreia* (manliness) and *fortitudo* (strength) and 2) strength of heart or endurance of faith and hope.

DAY SIX

Courage, Fear, and Hope

After the death of Moses the servant of the LORD, the LORD spoke to Joshua son of Nun, Moses' assistant, saying, "My servant Moses is dead. Now proceed to cross the Jordan, you and all this people,

> *into the land that I am giving to them, to the Israelites. Every place that the sole of your foot will tread upon I have given to you, as I promised to Moses. . . . No one shall be able to stand against you all the days of your life. As I was with Moses, so I will be with you; I will not fail you or forsake you. Be strong and courageous; for you shall put this people in possession of the land that I swore to their ancestors to give them. Only be strong and very courageous, being careful to act in accordance with all the law that my servant Moses commanded you; do not turn from it to the right hand or to the left, so that you may be successful wherever you go. . . . For then you shall make your way prosperous, and then you shall be successful. I hereby command you: Be strong and courageous; do not be frightened or dismayed, for the LORD your God is with you wherever you go."*
>
> —Joshua 1:1-3, 5-9

Many people make the mistake of believing that in order to have courage, you cannot have fear. This is a false and unfortunate idea that often hinders us from acting. There is a story about two officers in the Confederate army who were in the midst of a raging and bloody battle. Seeing the obvious terror on the face of the other man, the first officer turned to his comrade and said, "Sir, if I were as afraid as you I'd be ashamed to be an officer in this army." Whereby the second officer replied, "Sir, if you were as afraid as I, you would have left the battlefield by now."

Courage exists in the midst of our fear. Lewis B. Smedes has said that courage is at home in the frightened heart. The Bible repeatedly emphasizes this message. Joshua, one of the bravest characters in the Old Testament, had the responsibility of leading the Israelites into the promised land. Moses has died and God is instructing Joshua about his new responsibilities of leadership. In the midst of his promises of a new homeland, God reminds Joshua to be strong and courageous. Now this fact alone doesn't say much; however, when we look closely, we realize that God has to tell Joshua to be strong and courageous no less than three times. Joshua must have been afraid or God would not have had to remind him to be courageous so many times. Yet here is the crux. God is not asking for blind courage. Rather, God asks for the courage that comes from knowing that God will be with Joshua wherever he goes, that God will not fail or forsake him. God supports Joshua in his fear, empowers him to act and uses him for his purposes. God does no less with us.

We mentioned yesterday that the fear we face can be physical, mental, moral, emotional, or spiritual. Therefore, courage is required of us in all areas of our lives. Yet, the question of where we get the courage we need to act despite our fear remains. We believe that it is hope that gives us the courage to act when we are afraid. Our lives are lived with fear and hope, often experienced at the same time. In *A Pretty Good Person*, Lewis B. Smedes writes, "Fear lurks behind hope the way the dark side of the moon lurks behind its shining face. And hope answers fear the way the sun answers the darkness of the night." Without hope, all courage dies. We gain courage for living, all of our living, when we have the hope that life will win. One observation of historians is that people only change their world when they have hope that things can get better. Revolts against dictatorships occur not because people are oppressed; rather, oppressed people revolt against dictatorships because they have hope that freedom is available for them.

Hope is what gives us the courage to do the things we are afraid of doing because hope is faith that we will prevail; and this faith gives us the power to be victorious. Yet hope is not magical. It doesn't take away all the evil from the world. In the movie *Braveheart*, Mel Gibson plays a man who bravely leads a Scot movement of revolt against England during the twelfth century. The movement has only been partially successful, and toward the end of the movie he is awaiting death at the hands of a torturous executioner. In a moving scene, he is alone in his cell, awaiting the escort to take him to the executioner's block in the town square. He is visibly afraid, trembling and sweating and pacing. Finally, in a last prayer, he asks God simply to help him to die well. The hope that gives him courage to face the executioner is not the hope that he will somehow be spared, it is the hope of Joshua: that God will not forsake him, but will be with him in his suffering and that through his death others might be encouraged to fight on.

While we all hope for the healing of the world and our triumph over evil, as Christians our hope is deeper even than that; for we know that God has already triumphed over evil through the cross and is even now healing our broken and hurting world. When our fear tells us that we are alone, hope tells us that God is still here and that he is on our side. Hope tells us that God is on the side of life, not death; the side of love, not hate; the side of healing, not brokenness; the side of joy, not misery; the side of peace, not war. As Christians our hope is seen at its zenith in the resurrection of Jesus Christ. For in the resurrection we have our hope in the ultimate victory of God. With this hope, we can live with courage, even sacrifice, and risk our lives for others and for the sake of justice and righteousness.

REFLECTING AND RECORDING

Spend a few minutes reflecting on this truth: *Hope is what gives us courage to do the things we are afraid of doing because hope is faith we will prevail.*

Have you had a personal experience or have you seen a situation which verifies this truth? Describe that experience or situation.

The above truth includes the notion that "hope is faith we will prevail." Spend some time considering the possibility of hope giving us courage to do the things we may be afraid of doing even when we don't have faith that we will prevail—at least in our experience and in our lifetime.

DURING THE DAY

Continue observing the two kinds of courage illumined yesterday.

DAY SEVEN

Courage, Will, and Freedom

Soon Daniel distinguished himself above all the other presidents and satraps because an excellent spirit was in him, and the king planned to appoint him over the whole kingdom. So the presidents and the satraps tried to find grounds for complaint against Daniel in connection with the kingdom. But they could find no grounds for complaint or any corruption, because he was faithful, and no negligence or corruption could be found in him. The men said, "We shall not find any ground for complaint against this Daniel unless we find it in connection with the law of his God." So the presidents and the satraps conspired and came to the king and said to him, "O King Darius, live forever! All the presidents of the kingdom, the prefects and the satraps, the counselors and governors are agreed that the king should establish an ordinance and enforce an interdict, that whoever prays to anyone, divine or human, for thirty days, except to you, O king, shall be thrown into a den of lions. Now, O king, establish the interdict and sign the document, so that it cannot be changed, according to the laws of the Medes and Persians, which cannot be revoked." Therefore King Darius signed the document and interdict. Although Daniel knew that the document had been signed, he continued to go to his house, which had windows in its upper room open toward Jerusalem, and to get down on his knees three times a day to pray to his God and praise him, just as he had done previously.

—Daniel 6:3-10

My children have a book, *The Story of Ruby Bridges*, written by Robert Coles and illustrated by George Ford. It's the moving story of a little girl named Ruby Bridges who was the first black child to attend an all-white elementary school in New Orleans, Louisiana. Each day, escorted by federal marshals, she would walk to school, through mobs of angry people shouting and spitting at her. Each day, on her way to school, a few blocks before she got there, and again on her way home, a few blocks after she left, she would stop and pray for the crowd. In her prayer young Ruby asked God to forgive the angry mob.

On Day Five we talked about courage as being more than physical bravery, but being a power of the heart. On Day Six we talked about hope that enables us to act despite our fear. Yet the question remains of how courage, this power of our hearts, gets into us. How is it that Daniel had the courage to continue to pray after it became outlawed? How is it that little Ruby Bridges had the courage, not only to be the only black child to attend an all-white school day after day, but to pray for those who were persecuting her? We believe that the answer to this question is that courage is a strength of the heart that resides in our will. Daniel used his will to break the law and continue praying. Ruby exercised her will, in determining that each day she would go to school and that each day she would pray.

Courage is an act of the will; and as an act of the will it is the exercise of choice. We choose to be courageous or not be courageous. We make a deliberate effort of our will to act according to our principles. If he had chosen to, Daniel could have obeyed the edict. He could have stopped praying. If they had chosen to, the satraps and presidents could have respected Daniel for the committed Jew that he was. If she had chosen to, Ruby could have decided to stay home. If they had chosen to, those in the mob who taunted her could have been supportive, could have chosen not to gather, could have chosen to send their own children to school along with Ruby. Each person makes choices, exercises his or her will in ways that show courage or cowardice.

This may sound like an intimidating word; but in actuality it is quite liberating. We don't have to be conformed to this world. Because courage is an act of the will, it will not always be seen in the same way. Courage can, in fact, be shown in many different ways. You can show courage by moving forward, or by moving back. You can show courage by speaking out, or by remaining quiet. You can show courage by bearing your burdens or by throwing them off. You can show courage by dying for a good cause or by living for a good cause. Simply put, you can show courage by saying yes or by saying no.

Courage is a power of the will that keeps us free. Courage exercised through our will moves us closer to our true selves. Wisdom is a necessary ingredient of courage at this point. Without wisdom, using our will to make choices may or may not be courageous. If we always say no, we are not necessarily courageous; rather we may be simply stubborn. If we always say yes, we are merely a reflection of our culture. We need wisdom to discern what the courageous choices will be in our lives; wisdom informs us about when to say yes and when to say no.

Life will always provide us with opportunities for courage or cowardice. Our lives are filled with choice after choice after choice; so it is important for us to foster areas of our lives that encourage courageous choices. We must develop and strengthen our wills so that we will be up to the challenge of exercising our wills courageously.

Two ways that courage can be fostered in our lives are through stories and community. Plato told his students that the way to teach courage to children was to tell them stories. God knew this and thus instructed the Hebrews to tell the stories of the faith over and over to their children. As Israelite children grew, they heard, again and again, how God handed their people out of bondage and into freedom, how God had guided them and blessed them, and how God had remained faithful even when they had not.

Lewis B. Smedes tells of a man named Sandor Ungvari, an elderly Hungarian scholar. He wrote a book called *Life and Death of Hungarian Nazism* that marked him for trouble when the Nazi armies invaded Hungary in 1939. He was arrested, sentenced, tortured; but he survived. Then the Communists came. They assumed that since he had been tortured by the Nazis he would support the new regime; but they were wrong. Sandor organized an underground resistance movement composed of fellow intellectuals. For this he was arrested and charged with sixty counts of spying for the United States. He was sentenced to death by hanging.

Fortunately, Sandor's lawyer was able to negotiate his sentence. Instead of hanging he was sentenced to eight years in the notorious Gherla prison, an island prison with the reputation that no one left alive. With the help of three nationalist guards, Sandor was able to escape. Outside the walls, he swam across the freezing Szamos River and walked at night, from village to village, locating a pastor in each place who would send him on to the pastor in the next town. Through this pastoral underground, he made it to the Austrian border and freedom. Reflecting on the question, "Why did you do it? Why did you resist so openly?" Sandor replied, "It was my family. They were all resisters, all of them, right from the beginning—from Janos Ungvari, a Magyar galley slave, to Andreas Ungvari, who was a leader in the Hungarian Reformation. I heard their stories over and over all my childhood days. With such family memories, could I do anything else?"

Courage comes into our hearts almost by osmosis when we hear and rehear stories of courage: the remarkable stories of our faith, the extraordinary stories of others. Courage grows and forms within us even as ordinary parents pass on to their children the stories of heroes in their own families.

Our wills must be formed to include the strength of courage. That can occur through story-telling; and it is fostered through community. Courage is an individual thing; no one can have courage for us; yet, behind each courageous person stands a community of people. While courage may be singular, it is also infectious. When we are close to others, courage spreads. When we are part of a community that is grounded on trust—that provides for us the encouragement and support we need in times of crisis—then courage is fostered. Certainly it takes courage simply to be a part of an intimate community. It takes courage to relate to others honestly and openly, to make ourselves vulnerable and to respond with sensitivity to the unguarded openness of others. Yet, once we have the courage to be part of a real community, we are surprised to find a new source of courage beyond ourselves, hope. Community is the home of hope; and as we already know, hope is the source of courage.

REFLECTING AND RECORDING

Do you know some stories of courage out of your family or community? Think about it. List as many as come to your mind, simply giving the name of a person or writing a sentence that will identify the story.

Look at each of the stories. What role did faith, hope and will/choice play in each?

Is one of the stories yours? If not, identify in your memory an occasion when you exercised courage. Make enough notes to get the story clearly in mind.

Now spend a few minutes thinking about the role faith, hope and will/choice played in your personal courage story.

Spend whatever time you can spare now thinking about how the above experiences of courage were fostered and sustained by community.

DURING THE DAY

Review the experiences of courage you recorded above. If you know persons involved in them, write them a letter or call them on the phone, affirming them in their witness to you.

GROUP MEETING FOR WEEK TWO

Introduction

Participation in a group such as this is a covenant relationship. You will profit most as you keep the daily discipline of the thirty-minute period and as you faithfully attend these weekly meetings. Do not feel guilty if you have to miss a day in the workbook or be discouraged if you are not able to give the full thirty minutes in daily discipline. Don't hesitate sharing that with the group. We may learn something about ourselves as we share. We may discover, for instance, that we are unconsciously afraid of dealing with the content of a particular day because of what is required and what it reveals about us. Be patient with yourself and always be open to what God may be seeking to teach you.

Our growth, in part, hinges upon our group participation, so share as openly and honestly as you can. Listen to what persons are saying. Sometimes there is meaning beyond the surface of their words which you may pick up if you are attentive.

Being a sensitive participant in this fashion is important. Responding immediately to the feelings we pick up is also crucial. Sometimes it is important for the group to focus its entire attention upon a particular individual as mentioned before. If some need or concern is expressed, it may be appropriate for the leader to ask the group to enter into a brief period of special prayer for the persons or concerns revealed. Participants should not always depend upon the leader for this kind of sensitivity, for the leader may miss it. Even if you aren't the leader, don't hesitate to ask the group to join you in special prayer. This praying may be silent, or some person may wish to lead the group in prayer.

Remember, you have a contribution to make to the group. What you consider trivial or unimportant may be just what another person needs to hear. We are not seeking to be profound but simply to share our experience.

Sharing Together

Note: It may not be possible in your time frame to use all the suggestions provided each week. The leader should select what will be most beneficial to the group. It is important that the leader be thoroughly familiar with these suggestions in order to move through them selectively according to the direction in which the group is moving and according to the time available. The leader should plan ahead, but do not hesitate to change your plan according to the nature of the sharing taking place and the needs that emerge.

1. Open your time together with the leader offering a brief prayer of thanksgiving for the opportunity of sharing with the group and petitions for openness in sharing and loving response to each other.

2. Invite someone to read the last paragraph preceding Reflecting and Recording on Day Seven, page 51.

3. Let each person share either the most meaningful or the most difficult day in this week's workbook adventure.

4. Invite two persons to describe briefly the persons that came to their mind as they pondered the image of "a tree planted by streams of water."

5. Spend five to eight minutes discussing virtues as disciplines we exercise in our quest for goodness.

6. The two blocks to truth (wisdom) are ignorance and ideology. Spend ten to twelve minutes discussing this assertion: *Ignorance is simply not knowing; it is not having wisdom because we do not know the truth. In contrast, ideology is the twisting of truth for the purpose of power; we do not have wisdom because we have altered the truth for our own purposes.* Don't keep the discussions simply intellectual. Look at your community and see if there are warring forces, each claming to have the truth.

7. Invite a couple of persons to share an experience of wisdom that transcended "human thinking" and knowledge, or an occasion when they were given a wisdom not their own.

8. Accepting the truth that wisdom recognizes there are moral principles that are always right, and breaking them is always wrong, spend six to ten minutes naming those moral principles which are always right and discussing why

you think they are. Include in your discussion occasions in your life which have proven that breaking these principles is always wrong.

9. Spend four to six minutes sharing your ideas about courage. What new insight or understanding did you receive from your study and reflection this week? What does it mean to say that *without hope, all courage dies. We gain courage for living, when we have hope that life will win?*

10. Invite someone to share an experience of courage to do something she was afraid to do because hope gave her the faith that she could prevail.

11. Invite someone to share a time of courage to attempt something he was afraid of doing even though he didn't have faith that he would prevail.

12. Spend as much time as you have left telling your family or community stories of courage, noting the roles that faith, hope and will/choice played in each.

Praying Together

The effectiveness of this group and the quality of relationship will be enhanced by a commitment to pray for one another by name each day. If you have pictures of one another, put these pictures facedown on a table and let each person select a picture. This person will be the focus of special prayer for the week. Bring the photos back next week, shuffle them, and draw again. Continue this throughout your pilgrimage together. Looking at a person's picture as you pray for that person will add meaning. Having the picture will also remind you that you are to give special prayer attention to this person during the week.

1. Praying corporately each week is a special ministry. Take some time now for a period of verbal prayer. Rehearse some of the sharing that has taken place. Now allow each person to mention any special needs he or she wishes to share with the entire group. A good pattern is to ask for a period of prayer after each need is mentioned. There may be silent prayer by the entire group, or someone may offer a brief two-or-three-sentence verbal prayer.

2. Close your time by praying together The Lord's Prayer. As you pray remember that you are linking yourselves with all Christians of all time in universal praise, confession, thanksgiving, and intercession.

Week Three

Justice and Temperance

Justice: Giving Each Person His or Her Due

So justice is driven back, and righteousness stands at a distance; truth has stumbled in the streets, honesty cannot enter. Truth is nowhere to be found, and whoever shuns evil becomes a prey. The LORD looked and was displeased that there was no justice. He saw that there was no one, and he was appalled that there was no one to intervene.

—Isaiah 59:14-16, NIV

In 1963, our family moved from Mississippi to California because of the racial tension at that time and in that place. We were supportive of the Civil Rights Movement and Martin Luther King, Jr.; unfortunately, the church was not.

Things have changed a lot since then; certainly on the surface. But deep down, have they really changed? What do we feel at the core of our beings and how do those feelings creep out now and then to determine our attitudes, relationships and actions? At my ordination service in 1996, Bishop Woodie White, an African-American, said that he is welcomed in many churches because he's the bishop. However, if he were to be appointed as pastor, many of those same churches wouldn't accept him because he is black. I suppose this is what we mean when we say the more things change the more they stay the same. But we must not make the mistake of thinking that it's someone else's problem, or that it's only a matter of race. It has been our experience in most of the places we have lived that there are at least a few people everywhere that aren't really comfortable with a woman in the pulpit.

We have a crisis today, just like the one Isaiah was confronting when he spoke those incriminating words to Israel. It's a crisis of justice. It's a quiet crisis, not always obvious on the surface; but it's there, growing ever more ominous. Occasionally, this crisis rears its ugly head—a young black couple is slain simply because of the color of their skin; an entire village is massacred because they are of another cultural group—but then the crisis seems to disappear, sinking back down to the depths of our being, simmering ominously until it boils up again.

You may not have connected this crisis with justice. We who live in the United States seem to have a false sense of the strength of this virtue. Our country was founded on the principle of "liberty and justice for all"; therefore, we like to think of the United States as a model of equality and opportunity. We are not living under a formal system of apartheid. We are convinced that anyone can come here to pursue "the American dream." We reassure ourselves that justice is alive and well here at home. But justice is not alive and well, not here in the United States, nor anywhere else in the world. How easily the modern-day prophet might cry out with Isaiah: "Justice is driven back, and righteousness stands at a distance; truth has stumbled in the streets." And God must certainly be appalled that there is no one to intervene for the sake of righteousness.

Justice has to do with what we feel, how we relate to one another, what we value, the priorities we set. As we will see during Week Four, justice has to do with our faith; and as we will see during Week Five, at its very center, justice has to do with love. In the classical sense of Plato and Aristotle, justice is simply a matter of giving each person his or her due. It is a civic virtue that a civil society depends upon. It sounds simple enough—giving each person his or her due—but history has shown it to be an elusive and difficult concept to put into practice. As Christians, particularly, it helps us to remember that our duty to act justly is derived from the requirement to be just because justice is an attribute of God. When we fail "to give each person his or her due," when we ignore the calls of those who are suffering injustice, we are ignoring the cry and supplication of God.

REFLECTING AND RECORDING

Ponder for a few minutes the definition of justice as giving each person his or her due.

Do you know a person who is not getting his or her due? Name that person here.

What is going on with this person? Is he/she being denied his/her due by family? by work? by the larger social system?

Are there persons as a group in your community, town, city, who are not receiving their due? Name this group here.

How are these persons being denied "their due"? What are the justice issues?

DURING THE DAY

As you observe life around you today and this week, deliberately try to see if there are persons who are not receiving their due.

DAY TWO

Justice Is a Natural Grace Marred by Sin

This is the covenant that I will make with the house of Israel after those days, says the LORD: I will put my law within them, and I will write it on their hearts; and I will be their God, and they shall be my people. No longer shall they teach one another, or say to each other, "Know the LORD," for they shall all know me, from the least of them to the greatest, says the LORD; for I will forgive their iniquity, and remember their sin no more.
—Jeremiah 31:33-34

One of the blessings God has given all of humanity is an intrinsic sense of justice. It is a natural grace that God freely gives to all people. God created each of us with a finely tuned mechanism that senses when things are unfair. Though not fully realized, God's law is within us. God has written it on our hearts. Over the years people have referred to it as our "moral compass." It's our built-in guide to "rightness" and "oughtness." To a certain extent, all of us instinctively know what is right and wrong.

In his book, *The Jekyll and Hyde Syndrome*, Stephen Shoemaker offered another way of looking at justice. He talked about a kind of "fairness meter." Within each of us is the ability to measure fairness, a meter, or indicator if you will. Originally God created our fairness indicators so that they were sensitive to all types of fairness, whether we were treating others fairly and whether we were being treated fairly. Of course, like most things God created, over the years we have messed it up. That's what we call sin! Sin entered our lives and tinkered with that finely-tuned mechanism. Now, when other people are wronged before our very eyes, the meter barely registers a tiny blip and there may be only a hint of moral outrage. But watch out if we are the persons being wronged! The indicator sounds off louder than a fire alarm. Unfortunately, because of sin, not only is the indicator no longer sensitive to justice for others, a subtle dysfunction is at work. No longer is the fairness indicator very good at telling us whether we are really being wronged. It can't help us discern whether we just think we're being wronged.

It's much like the two little boys who went to the dentist one day and waited until all the patients had been seen. When the dentist came out, the older boy spoke up, "Doctor, I want a tooth taken out, and I don't want any gas and I don't want it deadened because we're in a hurry." The dentist was very impressed and smiled at the little boy and said, "Well, you're a very brave young man. You want a tooth pulled but you don't want any gas and you don't want it deadened." And the little boy said, "That's right, 'cause we're in a hurry." "Well, okay," said the doctor, "but first, which tooth is it?" And the little boy turned to his smaller buddy and said, "Show him your tooth, Albert!"

This is the way our fairness indicators are calibrated. We don't mind pain or mistreatment, as long as it's not our own. When others suffer under the strains of injustice and oppression, our sense of outrage is never completely kindled. However, if it is us, or someone in our group, then the matter takes on grave importance. Recalibrating our fairness indicators, getting them back into good working order, is the goal of kindling the virtue of justice.

REFLECTING AND RECORDING

Yesterday, we reflected on the classical definition of justice: giving each person his or her due. Today we press the justice issue at a more personal level. How finely tuned do you believe your "fairness indicator" to be? Spend just a minute or two thinking about how sensitive you are to things not being right or just. When was the last time you felt you were treated unjustly? Make some notes briefly describing that experience—giving name, circumstances, emotions you felt, and outcome.

When was the last time you observed that someone else was being treated unjustly? Name the occasion and make some notes about what was actually going on, who was involved, what happened, what was the outcome?

Test your *fairness indicator* by the two incidents above. How much pain or outrage did you feel in each case? What kind of protest did you make in each case?

DURING THE DAY

As you move through the day, remain aware of the calibration of your "fairness indicator." Is it sensing only personal injustice, or is it sounding off for others as well?

DAY THREE

Biblical Justice

I will make justice the measuring line and righteousness the plumb line.

—Isaiah 28:17, NIV

While the classical idea of justice, giving each person his or her due, is important, it only scratches the surface of what justice actually means. The biblical sense of justice, what we call righteousness, goes much deeper. It is easy to think that Judaism's greatest contribution is the notion of monotheism.

> *The Shema is the first word of the Hebrew sentence:* Shema Yisroel Adonoi Elohaynu Adonoi Echod. *Translated it means:* "Hear, O Isreal: The Lord Our God, The Lord Is One." *This is the watchword, the motto, and the foundation of the Jewish faith. It is the first prayer that the Jewish child learns to utter. It is the last prayer the dying Jew repeats before he yields his soul to God. Historically, the Shema was repeated in every crisis. It is the Jewish affirmation of faith in God.*

—Silverman, p. 30

Siliverman reminds us, hower, that to think of monotheism as the greatest contri-bution of Judaism is a mistake.

> *The greatest contribution of Judaism is not the belief in one God—* monotheism—*but rather the belief in* ethical *monotheism—one moral God who demands morality from those who worship Him. The scriptural keynote of this divine imitation is sounded in Lev. 19:2:"Ye shall be holy; for I the* LORD *your God am holy."*
>
> *The rabbis amplified this by the following comment:"Even as He is merciful, so be thou merciful; even as He clothes the naked, buries the dead, and dispenses charity to all, do thou likewise."*
>
> —Silverman, pp. 34-35

Thus, while in the classical sense justice begins with the individual, in the bib-lical sense, justice begins with God.

Classical justice, particularly as it has come to be understood in modern times, has a pronounced legal flavor to it. It is concerned with the individual and his or her rights within the context of society. Biblical justice, however, has far more of a relational flavor. It is concerned with what goes on among people and nations as well as the power of God in our life and history. Righteousness is connected with the biblical notion of justice. "But the LORD of hosts shall be exalted in judgment, and God who is holy shall be hallowed in righteousness" (Isa. 5:16, NKJV).

Righteousness focuses on the power of God that sets things right and heals relationships, communities, nations, and the world. "Thus says the LORD: 'Keep jus-tice, and do righteousness, for My salvation is about to come, and My righteous-ness to be revealed' " (Isa. 56:1, NKJV). Where classical justice emphasizes the exte-rior dimension, how individuals are related to and exist within society, righteous-ness emphasizes both the exterior and the interior dimensions. Righteousness is concerned not only with the individual's relationship with society, but the indi-vidual's relationship to God. Thus, while we usually speak about justice in social terms, when speaking about righteousness, we must speak of personal right-eousness as well as social righteousness. These two dimensions of righteousness, personal and social, are necessary if we are to gain a full understanding of bibli-cal justice. They are necessary not only for our understanding, but in order for the power of God's righteousness to work in us and through us to heal relationships, communities, and the world.

One of the most telling illustrations of the difference between the secular and biblical senses of justice is seen in the way we speak about it. While in secular society we talk about "getting justice," the Bible speaks of "doing justice." One of the Proverbs puts it into perspective:

> *To do righteousness and justice is more acceptable to the* LORD *than sacrifice.*
>
> —Proverbs 21:3

There is a story in the Jewish Talmud that answers the question, "How may man work for God and demonstrate his love?" A king's subjects came to him and said:

> *"Oh, our King, we would show our love for thee. What shall we say unto thee? What gifts may we give thee?"*
>
> *The king answered: "My subjects, I am grateful for your goodness in coming before me to show your love. But what words shall you utter? I know the sentiments of your hearts. What gifts may you give me? Am I not the king, the ruler of the entire realm? If you would show your love for me, attend to my words. I have children, and I cherish them dearly. If you would show your love for me, then go forth and serve my children."*
>
> *When we come before God, the King of all Kings, to express our love by words and gifts alone, will this be acceptable before Him? We may imagine that God responds by saying: "I am grateful for the expressions of your love, but do I not know the sentiments of your hearts, both the hidden and the revealed? What gifts may you give to Me? Am I not the Ruler of heaven and earth? If you would show your love for Me, the Father, then go forth and serve My children."*
>
> —Silverman, p. 33

We "do justice" when we work to set things right or maintain what is already right. This involves our personal lives as well as our communal lives. At its very core, justice refers to love made manifest in spirit and action. We are acting justly, and we show our love of God the Father, by loving kindness and service to God's children. We will consider this more tomorrow.

REFLECTING AND RECORDING

Spend a few minutes examining your life-stance. Are you more interested in *getting* justice than in *doing* justice?

Describe the last experience you had that involved an effort to do justice.

DURING THE DAY

Be attuned to opportunities to do justice. Act on them.

DAY FOUR

Personal and Social Righteousness

This is how we know what love is: Christ gave his life for us. We too, then, ought to give our lives for others! If we are rich and see others in need, yet close our hearts against them, how can we claim that we love God? My children, our love should not be just words and talk; it must be true love, which shows itself in action.
—1 John 3:16-18, TEV

At its very core, righteousness has to do with love. Love expands our hearts. It deepens our compassion and heightens our sensitivities. Therefore, if we exercise the virtue of love, justice and righteousness will follow naturally in its wake. In strengthening our capacity to love, we strengthen and encourage righteousness within ourselves. Then, when we respond to God's love for us with love for each other, justice takes care of itself. We all know this is easier said than done. If it were as simple as it sounds, my family never would have had to leave Mississippi. But we all know that's not how it is. It's definitely not like that outside of the church; and unfortunately, it's not even like that inside the church. So where do we begin?

We begin with ourselves. Social righteousness cannot be achieved without personal righteousness as its foundation. Yet personal righteousness does not mean *private* righteousness. The values to which we commit ourselves in our personal lives must emanate outward from us to the world. Only then will our love be more than words and talk; it will be true love, which shows itself in action. When our love is made manifest in action, then the prophet Amos' word will be true: Justice will "roll down like waters, and righteousness like an everflowing stream" (Amos 5:24).

The love that we speak of is more than ritualistic kindness. Amos was talking about an everflowing stream, not short spurts or trickles here and there. A bonus at Christmas is no substitute for a living wage. A homeless shelter is not a legitimate replacement for affordable housing. Short bursts of compassion in response to situational needs such as famine or disaster are not an adequate alternative to ongoing support and development.

The rolling waters of justice depend on our personal commitment to righteousness. We are to be the everflowing stream, through our living out of the Ten Commandments, through our commitment to treating others as we would want them to treat us, through our loving of neighbors as we love ourselves. When we become the everflowing stream, rather than trickling in fits and starts, the marks of God's righteousness will be seen in our world: justice that is blind to color or gender, protection for the weak, fairness in the courts, the opportunity for honest work for all who are willing, greater care of the earth. It is the virtue of love that must be translated into action if righteousness, both personal and social, is to prevail. During Week Five, we will be exploring the virtue of love at greater depth; for now, however, we want to focus on three important marks of personal and social holiness: truth-telling, forgiveness, and promise-keeping.

Truthfulness is a dying art. Recall the striking image of Isaiah at which we looked on Day One of this week: "Truth has stumbled in the streets, honesty cannot enter" (Isa. 59:14, NIV). A sociologist once estimated that the average American tells *200 lies* a day. The norms of politeness that order our society even encourage lying. The extent of the crisis in truth-telling was illustrated comically in the 1997 movie *Liar, Liar*. The main character, played by Jim Carrey, was an habitual liar. He never told the truth; in fact you wondered if he were capable of telling the truth. A dramatic thing happened. He lied to his son, assuring him that he would be with him for a special birthday celebration. When his father didn't show up, the sad little boy made his birthday wish—that his father would be unable to lie for twenty-four hours. The wish comes true and the movie unfolds with one scene after another highlighting Carrey in various awkward and funny situations because of his required truth-telling.

As Christians we often like to think that we are the truthtellers. Unfortunately, however, that is not always the case. H. Stephen Shoemaker cites an article published in the *Louisville Times* 1984 that states that Gallup polls have found that "there is very little difference found in the behavior of the churched and unchurched on a wide range of issues, including lying, cheating, and stealing"(page 143).

Yet, truth-telling is essential for healthy relationships. Wedges are driven into relationships when people lie. This is true not only in our relationships with other individuals, but in our relationship with God, in the relationships between various groups, and in relationships between governments and nations. Righteousness is the power of God that makes relationships healthy. Truth-telling is the deliberate act of the will that enhances our personal righteousness and makes us partners with God in doing justice in our world.

A second aspect of personal righteousness is forgiveness. Forgiveness is crucial to God's justice. Experiencing God's forgiveness in our own lives is the first step in experiencing God's justice. So too, if we are to be instruments of God's justice in the world, forgiveness must be a crucial part. If we are unable to forgive, we will continue to fight. This is true in our personal lives as much as it is in the lives of competing groups and nations. Witness all the racially-motivated and hate-instigated violence, as well as all the stockpiled weaponry lying in wait for destruction. We must decide to live by mercy or die. Forgiveness is the answer to the dilemma of war—war between nations, war between groups, war within families, war between persons.

Justice without mercy is too harsh; it is demanding and uncreative; it becomes life-denying rather than life-giving. Both justice and mercy are attributes of God. Therefore, justice without mercy is not God's justice at all. There is a story from The *Midrash* that tells of the integration of these attributes.

> *Justice and mercy are also attributes of God. How does God exercise these divine attributes? The case is like that of a king who had some empty goblets. He said, "If I put hot water in them, they will burst. If I put cold water in, they will crack." So the king mixed cold and hot water together and poured it in, and the goblets were uninjured.*
>
> *Even so, God said, "If I create the world with the attribute of mercy alone, sin will multiply; if I create it with the attribute of justice alone, how can it endure? So I will create it with both, and thus it will endure."*
>
> —Silverman, p. 35

Reinhold Neibuhr once said that justice that is only justice soon degenerates into something that is less than justice. True righteousness, then, is justice tempered by mercy.

Finally, promise-keeping, like truth-telling, is necessary for the health of all types of relationships. If we do not hold ourselves accountable to the commitments we make to others, we have no reason to be surprised when others do not keep their commitments to us.

Isaiah spoke to the Israelites about their religiosity:

> *Is not this the fast that I choose: to loose the bonds of injustice, to undo the thongs of the yoke, to let the oppressed go free, and to break every yoke? Is it not to share your bread with the hungry, and bring the homeless poor into your house; when you see the naked, to cover them, and not to hide yourself from your own kin?*
>
> —Isaiah 58:6-7

If this is the task of justice, then we must stand as ones who are trustworthy to accomplish the task. If we do not stand with integrity, so that all who know us know that we are promise-keepers, then, how can it be that the hungry will trust that we will feed them, or the oppressed that we will loose their bonds?

Personal righteousness is a supreme act of the will, empowered by God. It takes effort—effort to tell the truth, effort to forgive others, effort to keep promises. Yet, if we rise to the challenge, our personal righteousness can affect others and thus be transformed into social righteousness.

This process of translating personal righteousness into social righteousness is not an easy task. There are many pitfalls that can entrap us and misdirect us; two are worth noting. The first is the assertion that one particular group is the instrument of God's righteousness. We can see this scenario being played out on our political stage. While God has always worked and continues to work in our lives and history, it is dangerous for a political party or any other group to claim that they are the instrument of God's righteousness. The Bible refers to this as blasphemy. The second pitfall is closely tied to the first and involves the church. When the church identifies God's will with the activity of a particular political party or group, they too are in a dangerous situation. This situation is spiritually dangerous because of the subtle sacrifice of religious freedom in favor of political religion. The Bible calls this idolatry.

Justice is the gift of God to us that evidences God's power to make things right, to heal relationships between persons, within communities and nations, and the world. When we commit ourselves to personal righteousness and become the everflowing stream, God's righteous power will become more evident and justice indeed will roll down like waters to refresh and renew our barren lives and land.

REFLECTING AND RECORDING

Can you think of particular groups which have been in the news in the past few weeks making the claim that they are the instrument of God's righteousness? How do we assess such claims? When do such claims become blasphemy?

There have been times when the church has defined herself so politically that she has been identified with the left wing of the Democratic party or the right wing of the Republican party. In what sense is this dangerous? In what sense is it idolatry?

Do you feel that you are expressing your commitment to justice and righteousness through your political involvements?

Page 67 lists three marks of personal righteousness. Recall briefly one experience which demonstrates one of the marks—preferably from your personal experience, but if not, an experience you shared in or know about. How was justice/righteousness expressed? Make enough notes to capture the experience.

Truth-telling

Forgiveness

Promise-keeping

DURING THE DAY

As you read the newspapers, watch television, and have conversation, pay attention to the overlap of politics and religion. What claims are being made? How do they harmonize with God's call to let justice roll down like waters and righteousness like an everflowing stream?

DAY FIVE

Nothing Overmuch

For this very reason, you must make every effort to support your faith with goodness, and goodness with knowledge, and knowledge with self-control, and self-control with endurance, and endurance with godliness, and godliness with mutual affection,

*and mutual affection with love. For if these things are yours and
are increasing among you, they keep you from being ineffective
and unfruitful in the knowledge of our Lord Jesus Christ.*

—2 Peter 1:5-8

Today we turn our attention to temperance. In our modern world, temperance is the virtue that seems to be the least popular and most ridiculed. Many of us, however, don't actually understand what is meant by the word temperance. In a nutshell, it simply means moderation. The ancient maxim was "nothing overmuch"; thus, rather than being viewed as the elimination of all our natural inclinations or "appetites," temperance was seen as the proper ordering of what is good within our natures. The maxim, nothing overmuch, applied then to temperance itself. Thus, temperance excluded prideful abstinence as well as joyless asceticism, and strove for a healthy balance.

Over time, philosophers and theologians have come to view temperance as one of the most important virtues. The Greeks believed it was necessary to produce a well-ordered soul, a well-balanced self, and a well-proportioned life. Plato wrote that temperance was the rational ordering of the soul that kept it free. If the soul is to remain free and not in bondage to a particular impulse or appetite, temperance is crucial. Aristotle even went so far as to assert that temperance was the prerequisite for all the other virtues. For instance, temperance was required to produce courage, because courage is the balance between cowardice and rashness.

The opposite of temperance, of the balance that we seek in our lives, is intemperance, or a lack of balance. The intemperate person is like a pot that is full of holes. It can never be satisfied because it can never be full. Intemperance occurs in two ways. One, part of the self rules the whole self. Examples of this would be alcoholism and other addictions. The addicted person is ruled by the part of the self that desires that to which it is addicted. There is no ordering of that desire in relation to the other needs and desires of the self. The addicted desire is all-consuming. While addiction is a good example of this first type of intemperance, we should not make the mistake of thinking that intemperance occurs only in these extremes. Whether it be the drive to succeed in a career which puts us in conflict with our commitments at home, or the desire to be everything for our families which often places us at odds with our desire for personal fulfillment, anyone who has ever been torn by competing desires has experienced periods of intemperance.

Intemperance is not merely the domination of the whole self by one part; it can also be a fragmentation of the self. When we do not truly know ourselves, we can become pulled in too many different directions. Rather than one excess ruining the whole, it is the excess of many things that pulls us apart. When our lives become filled with too many competing demands, we fall into the trap of intemperance. We are unable to find balance because we are unable to find our center, and order our lives around that center. Prioritizing becomes difficult and as a result we are pulled apart.

As we seek to find balance in our lives we must be careful to avoid confusing temperance with asceticism. Asceticism views the natural world as evil and thus demands abstinence. Temperance sees all creation as good, including our inner desires, but seeks to order those desires so that we remain free and productive.

The temperate person knows herself. She knows what is important and sets priorities and goals. The temperate person understands the idea of delayed gratification and is willing to make sacrifices for what he wants. Temperate people tend to make wise judgments about what to do and not do to in order to achieve their goals. They are willing to make choices and commitments as they seek to order their souls.

Temperance is the art of finding balance within yourself. It is a blessing when achieved and a burden when it is not. The balance of temperance will be different for each of us. For some, it may involve abstinence in a particular area, where for others it may involve a seeming indulgence. For us all, it involves prayer for discernment and hard work to balance and order our souls.

REFLECTING AND RECORDING

Think about the ancient maxim, "nothing overmuch." Do you find that to be a principle that you live by? Why or why not?

One way intemperance occurs is *one part of the self rules the whole self.* Examine your life. Is there one part of your self that is ruling your life? Name that part of the self.

Spend a few minutes reflecting on your need to cultivate temperance ("nothing overmuch") in relation to this dominant aspect of your self.

The other way the lack of temperance works in us is the fragmentation of the self: the excess of many things pulls us apart. Name two or three drives, appetites, habits, or personality traits that seek dominance in your life.

Spend a few minutes reflecting on how the practice of temperance could bring these into balance.

DURING THE DAY

As you move through this day, be aware of tendencies toward intemperance. Is there an area of your life that is dominating at the expense of balance? Do you need to say "No" more often?

DAY SIX

Christ-Centered and Spirit-Filled

But the fruit of the Spirit is love, joy, peace, patience, kindness, goodness, faithfulness, gentleness and self-control. Against such things there is no law. Those who belong to Christ Jesus have crucified the sinful nature with its passions and desires. Since we live by the Spirit, let us keep in step with the Spirit.
—Galatians 5:22-25, NIV

As we discovered when we explored the virtue of justice, the biblical notion of virtue draws upon and deepens the classical notion. The same holds true with temperance. Scripture raises the stakes of temperance, making it not only more demanding but more meaningful and rewarding as well. From the classical Greek perspective, temperance produces a well-ordered and well-proportioned soul. This is true of the biblical perspective as well; however, from the biblical perspective there is a goal to that order. The goal is love. Our souls are not simply to be well-ordered; they are to be well-ordered toward love, the love of God and the love of our neighbor. The order that we achieve through temperance is not for our own sake; although that is certainly a benefit. The order that comes to our souls through temperance is for the sake of God and our neighbor.

In classical Greek thinking, the mind conquers all problems; thus, the root of evil is ignorance. Reason is what saves us; therefore, temperance is the rational ordering that comes through an exercise of the mind. Christian temperance is, on the surface, quite similar; but it has a completely different foundation. The biblical notion of temperance asserts that it is not ignorance but sin, that distortion of our heart, that is the root of evil. Reason alone is unable to save us. Reason can fix ignorance, but it cannot fix sin. Only Christ can fix sin. Therefore, it is not reason that produces temperance, but the Holy Spirit that indwells us when we come into relationship with Jesus Christ. Temperance, then, is the living of a Spirit-filled, Christ-centered life.

Creating the balance that is temperance has always been a challenge; yet these days the challenge seems greater than ever. We live in an age where there are so many things competing for our time, attention, and energy that we can often become numb from stimulation overload. It is imperative that we find our center and order our lives around it.

As Christians, Christ is our center. He is the one to whom we look to provide the order for our souls. Taking on the yoke of Christ guards us against intemperance. When Christ is Lord of our lives, nothing else can be; when Christ is not Lord of our lives, anything and everything else will be. With Christ as our center we are oriented toward wholeness, which prevents the whole from being ruled by a part or from being fragmented by the excess of many things. With Christ as our center, the order that comes to our lives is oriented toward love. H. Stephen Shoemaker said it well:

> *You have been created in the image of Christ; He is your secret self, the truest truth about who you are. This real self gets overlaid by many layers of false selves; your true self stays a secret even from you. When you receive Christ and invite Him to be Savior, Lord, and Friend, you get in touch with your true self. Because you know who you are, the compulsions of the false self fade away. When Christ is Lord, then all the good desires and appetites God has given us find their rightful place and stay as good as God made them.*
> —Shoemaker, p. 157

Placing Christ at the center of our lives allows the Holy Spirit's power to move us toward temperance. It also makes us aware that temperance does not stem from the law. Paul wrote to the Galatians, "If you are led by the Spirit, you are not subject to the law." We cannot enforce temperance by strict rules and regulations. The law forces an ordering that is external rather than internal, and therefore is never successful for very long. The temperance that springs from a Spirit-filled, Christ-centered life is one of joyful obedience rather than grim obligation. Jesus said, "Come to me, all you that are weary and are carrying heavy burdens, and I will give you rest. Take my yoke upon you, and learn from me; for I am gentle and humble in heart, and you will find rest for your souls. For my yoke is easy, and my burden is light," (Matt. 11:28-30). Taking on the yoke of Christ, making him Lord of our life helps us to organize our life toward the love of God and neighbor. It is not a yoke of abstinence or a denial of life; it is a yoke that reorders our life so that we are able to experience the deep happiness, the blessedness, of which we spoke in Week One. With Christ as our center, we make decisions because of what is right for us, not by anyone else's law or rule. In this way we are able to live happily, freely and responsibly. We are able to live temperately, in joyful obedience, affirming the abundant life to which Christ has called us.

REFLECTING AND RECORDING

Today we said that temperance does not spring from law; we do not enforce temperance by rules and regulations, but by being led of the Spirit. Yesterday, in your reflecting and recording, you were asked to name a part of your self that was ruling the whole self. Look at that again in terms of "Spirit" and "law." Spend some time examining whether you have been seeking to "control" this part of your self by law or by Spirit.

In relation to this dominating aspect of self, what do you need to do to be more Christ-centered and Spirit-filled?

Look again at the drives, appetites, habits, and/or personality traits you named yesterday which are seeking dominance in your life. How might this be brought into harmony if you gave less attention to trying to control them and surrendered them to Christ, seeking to allow the Spirit to prevail, rather than your own will?

DURING THE DAY

Begin and move through this day with this prayer: "I want to live by the Spirit; help me, Lord, to keep in step with the Spirit."

Balance Is Good Enough

Yesterday we explored the need to place Christ at the center of our lives in order to become empowered by the Holy Spirit to lead a temperate life. Today we focus on some practical ramifications of that commitment. We can do that by looking at one of the wonderful stories of the Old Testament.

> *In the days when the judges ruled, there was a famine in the land, and a certain man of Bethlehem in Judah went to live in the country of Moab, he and his wife and two sons. The name of the man was Elimelech and the name of his wife Naomi, and the names of his two sons were Mahlon and Chilion; they were Ephrathites from Bethlehem in Judah. They went into the country of Moab and remained there. But Elimelech, the husband of Naomi, died; and she was left with her two sons. These took Moabite wives; the name of one was Orpah, and the name of the other Ruth. When they had lived there about ten years, both Mahlon and Chilion also died, so that the woman was left without her two sons and her husband.*
>
> *Then she started to return with daughters-in-law from the country of Moab, for she had heard . . . that the Lord had considered his people and given them food. . . . But Naomi said to her two daughters-in-law, "Go back each of you to your mother's house. May the Lord deal kindly with you, as you have dealt with the dead and with me. The Lord grant that you may find security, each of you in the house of your husband." Then she kissed them, and they wept aloud. They said to her, "No, we will return with you to your people." But Naomi said, "Turn back, my daughters, why will you go with me? Do I still have sons in my womb that they may become your husbands?" . . . Then they wept aloud again. Orpah kissed her mother-in-law, but Ruth clung to her.*
>
> *So she said, "See, your sister-in-law has gone back to her people and her gods; return after your sister-in-law." But Ruth said, "Do not press me to leave you or to turn back from following you! Where you go, I will go; Where you lodge, I will lodge; your people shall be my people, and your God my God. Where you die, I will die—there I will be buried. May the Lord do thus and so to me, and more as well, if even death parts me from you."*
>
> *When Naomi saw that she was determined to go with her,*

she said no more to her. So the two of them went on until they
came to Bethlehem.

—Ruth 1:1-6, 8-11, 14-19

What an amazing story of courage and commitment! Ruth is understandably the hero of the story; after all, she chose the dangerous prospect of leaving her homeland to follow Naomi. But as heroic as Ruth is, we do ourselves a disservice if we fail to take a look at the other, often neglected character in this story, Orpah. When Naomi suggests that Ruth and Orpah return to their families, Orpah does just that. It's a logical and rational choice. Widows in general were in a precarious position during Bible times. If they didn't have family to care for them, they were often times left out in the cold; and to be a widow in a foreign land added that much more fear and despair. So Orpah's decision seems dictated by common sense. The most logical and secure choice is for both Orpah and Ruth to return to the care of their families. But scripture says that what ought to have been an easy choice wasn't easy at all. Both women cried with sorrow and it takes Orpah a long time to decide.

In the end though, Ruth follows Naomi to Judah and Orpah returns home. We don't know what happens to Orpah after that. We can probably safely assume that when she rejoined her family she led a secure life.

Naturally, the church has presented Ruth as a model of strength and character, which is perfectly appropriate; but we also think that Orpah needs some renewed attention. We believe that as we seek to gain, or regain, as the case may be, the virtue of temperance, of balance in our lives, we need to look at both of these women.

Ruth followed; Orpah did not. There is obvious tension between those two choices just as there is with many of the choices we face throughout our lives. All of our choices are important, even the small ones; because they are intertwined with our faith. The nature of our faith will determine the decisions we make about our commitments; and the decisions we make about our commitments will determine the nature of our faith. But here is the rub. There will always be people out there that will hold up one of our choices as the only one we should take. This is true for both men and women; and it is true in all the areas of our life. As we confront the demands of life that pull us in varying directions, we need to remember that both Orpah and Ruth made courageous and good decisions. They did what was right for them; and each of us must do the same. If we must be the "Orpahs" in the eyes of a group that thinks we should be the Ruths, then so be it. We can't all be Ruths. And we can't be all Orpahs. We will never be able to be all things to all people. We are always going to have to make choices about how we live our lives.

Two areas in particular exemplify the extreme way we are forced to make our life choices: the areas of home and work. In these areas, our culture has created what we believe to be two false and competing choices and has offered these up as our only ones. Both are extremes. The first is *if you want it, you have to sac-*

rifice everything else to get it. This false choice has been offered to both men and women. For men, it is the dilemma in which they have always found themselves. Work has been and continues to be seen as the main and sometimes only source of meaning and identity for men. It is the place where they are supposed to find fulfillment and gratification. Other arenas of life, particularly home and family, have never been fully validated as appropriate places for men to turn for inner contentment and satisfaction. This "all or nothing" emphasis was also the mistake of the feminist movement of the 1970s. Women's "liberation" issued the call for women to catch up with men in the workplace; the rallying cry was "back to work!" and the image was "career woman." But in holding that up as the only choice, they denied the validity of a woman's ties to home.

The second false choice was offered up predominately to women in the 1980s. It was a boomerang to the extreme of Superwoman. This was the false choice that I fell prey to when I was coming of age. Women were told that they could be a supermom and a super career woman all at the same time. It was the "you can have it all" mentality, or the "have your cake and eat it too" way of thinking.

The bottom line, however, is that both of these extremes are false choices. Our lives are not like that. While society is still making it very difficult for men, many women are finding that it is possible to work without sacrificing everything else and denying their ties to home. But it is also true that we can't do everything without making some sacrifices. There will always be times when our commitments clash. More importantly, making the issue simply that of being employed versus being at home denies the complexity and need for balance in all areas of our life. We can be a stay-at-home parent or a retired person and still be up to our ears in competing commitments; being employed has nothing to do with it.

The fact that life is filled with conflicting commitments points to the necessity of temperance. If we are to apply the virtue of temperance to our life, we must develop an understanding of the concept of "good enough." "Good enough" is a concept that desperately needs to be rediscovered. We are encouraged by society and even by scripture to pursue excellence. Paul tells the Philippians, "if there is any excellence and if there is anything worthy of praise, think about these things" (Phil. 4:8). There is nothing wrong with striving to be the best you can be. We believe that excellence is a noble aspiration; but we also know that it can be a damaging notion as well. Many a family has suffered at the hands of a workaholic striving to the best employee there is. So we think there's a spot for the notion of "good enough."

When I first started seminary, I felt extremely stressed. I couldn't seem to find the right rhythm. Used to excellent grades and hard work, I naturally immediately reverted to my old study habits and expectations; but somehow it just didn't work the way it had in college. What I failed to realize was that my life was different than when I was in college; I was married, had a baby, and my husband was gone most of the time because of the demands of his surgical residency. I quickly discovered that I wasn't going to be able to be at the top of my class and be able to give my son, Nathan, the attention he needed. At the same time, I also recognized that I wasn't going to be able to be the "ideal" mother I had envisioned myself to be and successfully complete my master's degree. I had to find a balance. I had to find a way to be a good enough divinity school student and a good enough mother. I had to accept that being good enough at both of those things was okay. Ironically, what I discovered was that when I recognized the value of being good enough, I found my rhythm, I regained my balance and I actually began to excel both at home and at school.

Orpah knew about good enough. She made a decision, albeit a painful one, that was good enough for her. Each of us can claim that for ourselves as well. This is not just a "woman thing" either. All people need to claim "good enough." Rather than being torn in a million different directions, we need to make decisions that help us become good enough mothers and good enough fathers, good enough children, and good enough siblings, good enough employees and good enough volunteers, good enough friends and good enough citizens. When we find the balance of good enough, temperance reigns in our lives and we are free to excel.

REFLECTING AND RECORDING

Spend a few minutes thinking about Orpah. Have you stopped to consider her choice as a good one, worthy of affirmation?

Why have we made a hero of Ruth and discounted Orpah?

Where in your life is the center of competing demands? Name those clashing commitments.

Spend a few minutes thinking about the decisions and adjustments you would have to make to be "good enough" rather than "super" in these areas.

Write a prayer of confession, offering up to God your "all-or-nothing" stance—whatever in your life that has destructively driven you to be more than good enough.

DURING THE DAY

Test yourself in all your activities and relationships today: At what points are you driven needlessly to be super rather than good enough?

GROUP MEETING FOR WEEK THREE

Introduction

Two essential ingredients for a Christian fellowship are feedback and follow-up. Feedback is necessary to keep the group dynamic working positively for all participants. Follow-up is essential to express Christian concern and ministry.

The leader is primarily responsible for feedback in the group. All persons should be encouraged to share their feelings about how the group is functioning. Listening is crucial. To listen to another, as much as any other action, is a means of affirming that person. When we listen to another, we are saying, "You are important; I value you." It is also crucial to check out meaning in order that those who are sharing this pilgrimage may know that we really hear. We often mis-hear. "Are you saying ———?" is a good check question. It takes only a couple of persons in a group, who listen and give feedback in this fashion, to set the mood for the group.

Follow-up is the function of everyone. If we listen to what others are saying, we will discover needs and concerns beneath the surface, situations that deserve special prayer and attention. Make notes of these as the group shares. Follow up during the week with a telephone call, a written note of caring and encouragement, a visit. What distinguishes Christian fellowship is caring in action. "My, how those Christians love one another!" So follow up each week with others in the group.

Sharing Together

By this time, a significant amount of "knowing" exists in the group. Persons are feeling safe in the group, perhaps more willing to share. Still, there is no place for pressure. The leader, however, should be especially sensitive to those slow to share. Seek gently to coax them out. Every person is a gift to the group. The gift is fully given by sharing.

1. Spend five to ten minutes discussing the classic sense of justice: giving each person his or her due.

2. Invite two people to share their most memorable experience of being treated unfairly.

3. Reflect on these experiences. Are these experiences common? How do you feel when you see or hear of someone treated this way? What kind of response do you make?

4. Spend five to ten minutes discussing the difference between a classic understanding of justice and the more expansive biblical understanding (relational—as what goes on among people and nations as well as the power of God in our life and history.) Talk about *getting* justice and *doing* justice.

5. Invite anyone to share an example in your community where a person or a group of people are involved in an intentional ministry of *doing* justice.

6. On Day Five three marks of personal righteousness were discussed: truth-telling, forgiveness, and promise-keeping. Invite three persons to share an experience that demonstrates those marks.

7. Spend a few minutes talking about how we express our commitment to justice and righteousness through political activity. How does the church as a whole do this?

8. Spend five to ten minutes discussing temperance as the principle of "nothing overmuch." What are the most glaring examples of intemperance in our society?

9. Invite two or three persons to share their temptation of allowing *one part of the self to rule the whole self.*

10. Invite a person or two to share how he has found victory over some drive, appetite, habit, and/or personality trait by surrendering it to Christ, seeking to allow the Spirit to prevail, rather than seeking to control by his own will.

11. Spend what time you have left discussing Kim's testimony about "balance" in her life—her growing appreciation for Orpah, the notion that "good enough" rather than "super" is the balance we need.

Praying Together

1. Ask someone, maybe two persons, to volunteer to read the prayer of confession they wrote in their Reflecting and Recording time on Day Seven of this week.

2. The leader should take up the instant photos of the group, shuffle them, and let each person draw a new one, or draw a name written on a slip of paper.

3. Invite each member of the group to spend two minutes in quiet prayer for the person whose picture he or she has drawn, focusing on what the person has shared in this meeting.

4. Close this time of prayer inviting someone to pray for the areas in the community where there is a specific need for *doing* justice. Thank God for those who are giving themselves to justice ministries.

Week Four

The Theological Virtues: Faith and Hope

The Vital Connection

During the past three weeks, we have been dealing with the cardinal virtues: wisdom, courage, justice, and temperance. The word *cardinal* comes from Latin meaning hinge. Early philosophers contended that all other virtues hinge on these four. For the Christian, there is another perspective. To these four were added the theological virtues: faith, hope, and love. These have been seen as the classic virtues and the seven tools of the moral life. Paul named the theological virtues at the close of his magnificent Hymn of Love in 1 Corinthians 13: "And now faith, hope, and love abide, these three, and the greatest of these is love" (vs. 13).

During this week we will take a general look at faith with the conviction that faith is the tap root of any tree that is going to produce fruit of the Spirit. We will also glance briefly at hope. Love will be considered as we begin to look at Paul's listing of "fruit of the Spirit" in Week Five.

Paying attention to virtues, seeking to discipline ourselves in a good life, may appear to be an effort at salvation by works, which is foreign to Protestant Christianity. Paul addressed the issue in his letter to the Galatians:

> *You foolish Galatians! Who has bewitched you? It was before your eyes that Jesus Christ was publicly exhibited as crucified! The only thing I want to learn from you is this: Did you receive the Spirit by doing the works of the law or by believing what you heard? Are you so foolish? Having started with the Spirit, are you now ending with the flesh? Did you experience so much for nothing?—if is really was for nothing. Well then, does God supply you with the Spirit and work miracles among you by your doing the works of the law, or by your believing what you heard?*
>
> —Galatians 3:1-5

"You foolish Galatians!" Why was Paul so upset with the Galatians? Fire was in his pen as he begins this third chapter of his letter to them. He had preached the gospel to them . . . the gospel that he had experienced with saving power on the Damascus Road, and that had been clarified and refined in those years he spent in the desert as he sought to discern the fullness of what Christ had done for him and what he was being called to preach.

It had come clear, and now he was a slave to it: Jesus Christ, crucified for our sins, offering us forgiveness and salvation by the sheer gift of grace, God's gift. "Since all have sinned and fall short of the glory of God; they are now justified by

80

his grace as a gift, through the redemption that is in Christ Jesus, whom God put forward as a sacrifice of atonement by his blood, effective through faith" (Rom. 3:23-25). The Galatians had received that message, had experienced the joyous freedom that comes through the love and forgiveness which Christ had offered so extravagantly on the cross, which had freed Paul from his morbid preoccupation with the law and his mission of persecution against those who did not accept the rigid religious system of rules, regulations, and rituals. But something had happened. After Paul left this new Christian community in Galatia, continuing his mission of sharing the good news to the world, Judaizers came in to sound a discordant note and to sow seeds of confusion. Judaizers were early Christians who demanded that non-Jewish believers adopt Jewish customs as a criteria for salvation.

The Judaizers contended that pleasing God was a matter of doing what God said, and that meant primarily keeping the law and observing the rituals. If we do that, we will be holy and God will bless us, they said. Here was brought to focus the issue that concerned Paul throughout his ministry. He deals with it in almost all of his letters: the connection between faith and works.

If you don't read Paul's letters as a whole, you may find yourself asking, "Why did Paul preach so much against works? Didn't he want people to do good and be good?" The answer is in a bit of wisdom, captured in the maxim, "You are putting the cart before the horse." For Paul, you cannot begin with good works. That was the limitation of the law. No one could possibly keep the law. Keeping the law and doing good works could never save us. So, we begin with faith: faith in God who is righteous and whose righteousness is appropriated by us through faith. "For by grace you have been saved through faith, and this is not your own doing; it is the gift of God—not the result of works, so that no one may boast" (Eph. 2:8-9).

Persons who are content to offer God their own good works, works which flow out of their own will and power, will never be able to please God. God is holy. Do we think we, in our own power, can meet the standards of God's holiness? God is pure love. Do we think that our attitudes and actions can measure up to that standard of unfettered love? Paul insists that we can never be good enough, never holy enough, never loving enough to deserve God's grace. So, he concludes, God's grace is not earned or deserved, it is given. We receive it by faith.

Paul does not discount the meaning and necessity of good works. He follows the Ephesians 2 passage quoted above ("you have been saved by grace through faith not by the result of works") with this balancing word: "For we are what he has made us, created in Christ Jesus for good works, which God prepared beforehand to be our way of life" (vs. 10).

There is a vital connection between faith and works. Paul wants to make sure that we do not get the cart before the horse. We are saved by grace through faith, but we are "created in Christ Jesus for good works."

REFLECTING AND RECORDING

In light of our consideration of the four cardinal virtues during the past three weeks, spend some time looking at the way you have sought and practiced wisdom, courage, justice and temperance. Has this been an effort at good works, to "keep the law"?

Continue your reflection on good works and faith. How do you balance these in your life in seeking to please God? in your understanding of salvation?

DURING THE DAY

Examine your every action today. What is your motive?

DAY TWO

"And the Rock Was Christ"

Moreover, brethren, I do not want you to be unaware that all our fathers were under the cloud, all passed through the sea, all were baptized into Moses in the cloud and in the sea, all ate the same spiritual food, and all drank the same spiritual drink. For they drank of that spiritual Rock that followed them, and that Rock was Christ.

—1 Cor. 10:1-4, NKJV

Say what you will about the confusing, tumultuous years during the 1960s, musicians rose to great heights of insight. In their protest songs, they spoke the prophetic word. In many of their ballads, they diagnosed the human predicament, and sometimes offered a way of healing and reconciliation. In some haunting lines, Paul Simon did a masterful piece of diagnosis—a diagnosis that is still on target.

Simon spoke as a representative of all humankind in a song entitled "I am a Rock." In the verses of the song he talks about being behind a wall in a fortress "deep and mighty" that no one could penetrate; about having no need of friendship because friendship causes pain; about not wanting to awaken the love sleeping in his memory because if he had never loved he would have never cried; about the slumber of feelings that have died and he doesn't want to bring them to life; about being shielded in his armor, touching no one and no one touching him. In the song's chorus Simon named himself as a rock that felt no pain and an island that never cried.

Though an apt diagnosis, Paul Simon offered no prescription. But the Apostle Paul does. Either you will be a rock, or Jesus Christ will be your Rock.

In the scripture passage quoted above, Paul calls the Corinthian Christians' attention to Moses and the people of Israel coming out of captivity. He says of that event, "And all ate the same spiritual food, and all drank the same spiritual drink. For they drank from the spiritual Rock that followed them, and the Rock was Christ" (1 Cor. 10-3-4, NKJV).

What an image: "and the Rock was Christ."

This is the message of the New Testament. It is the heart of the Christian faith. God's grace for our salvation and "walk in newness of life" is given in and through his Son, Jesus—his life, teachings, death, and resurrection. Paul's depiction of this grace builds to a climax in Romans 5: "For while we were still weak, at the right time Christ died for the ungodly. . . . God proves his love for us in that while we still were sinners Christ died for us" (Rom. 5:6, 8).

On Day Two of Week One, we considered briefly the notion of justification: our being made right with God by grace. This grace is operative in our lives through faith. It is only by faith we receive God's gracious offer and accept Christ and his death for the forgiveness of our sin that we are pardoned and brought back into right relationship with God.

Go back to our image of the rock.

If you are a rock, you won't hurt, you won't cry, you won't feel pain because you won't love. You won't laugh either; you won't know joy and you won't live very much. But if Jesus is your Rock, you'll stand on it, and others will join you. Sometimes you'll laugh, sometimes you'll cry, sometimes you'll rejoice, sometimes you'll be very sad—but always you will work to live in the grace and love of God.

The Rock, Christ Jesus, will become the keystone for everything God wants to create in you and through you. And in some final time we will rejoice in the love of the One who gave us life, the One who loved us so much that he hung on a cross for us.

REFLECTING AND RECORDING

The essence of faith is trust. The Christian faith is more than believing; it is believing enough to trust. To have faith in Christ is to be willing to trust our lives to him.

Look at your spiritual pilgrimage, how you have come to faith in Christ and how you have grown in that faith. Write a brief spiritual biography, paying attention to how and to what degree you have trusted Christ.

DURING THE DAY

Find a way to talk to someone today about "the Rock" who is Christ, sharing your own experience of him.

DAY THREE

Faith Issues in Transformation

When Paul talks about our faith in Jesus Christ, he argues forcefully that not only are we forgiven, we are transformed. The past is forgiven and we are no longer in bondage to guilt and shame; neither are we victims to the ongoing power of sin. The witness of scripture is that sin is a conquered foe. Sin may remain in our lives, but it does not reign.

With this backdrop of the dynamic of our faith in Christ, we need to consider two limited and misleading extreme understandings. One extreme deals little with the salvation message of justification by grace through faith. We ignore the fact that we are helpless sinners in desperate need of grace, with no power to save ourselves, who, when left to our own devices, will continue to repeat the cycle of estrangement from God and works of injustice, unrighteousness, and all sorts of evil. The call is to be good and do good—"to do justice, love mercy, and walk humbly with God." We would like to do just that. We want and we seek to respond, but find ourselves unable to walk in the light very long. But when we fall back into our ways of selfishness, prejudice, lust, unbridled anger, self-protection, pride, gluttony—wanting more and more and needing more and more to be satisfied—we are discouraged and guilt-stricken. "Woe is me . . . who can live this life to which the church is calling me?"

The other limited and misleading extreme is an emphasis on the way of salvation that looks like this: Now that you have been saved, *you are in.* Turn your attention to your family, friends, and neighbors. Make sure they become Christians too. This is your primary task—witnessing and winning others.

I hope no one would diminish the opportunity and responsibility of every Christian to witness and seek to win others to Christ. Yet, if we make that the priority of every new Christian and do not emphasize that it is equally important to develop a lifestyle so dynamic and different that others would take note and say, "That's the kind of life I would like to live—how can I get it?" then we are betraying the gospel.

As we suggested on Day One of this week, there is a vital connection between the tree and its fruit: faith and works. Jesus spoke clearly about it.

> *No good tree bears bad fruit, nor again does a bad tree bear good fruit; for each tree is known by its own fruit. Figs are not gathered from thorns, nor are grapes picked from a bramble bush. The good person out of the good treasure of the heart produces good, and the evil person out of evil treasure produces evil; for it is out of the abundance of the heart that the mouth speaks.*
> —Luke 6:43-45

The prophet Isaiah gave a challenging picture in Isaiah 5:1-10. He tells of a vineyard which produced bad fruit. The owner spared no effort to make it produce the very best grapes. He removed the stones from the soil, turned the soil with a hoe, planted the best vines available, even built a tower to protect the vineyard from thieves. He was so hopeful that he hewed out of the rocky soil a trough for the juice to flow through. And he waited!

He was horrified. No full ripe grapes came from the well-cultivated vines . . . only wild grapes, perhaps small, sour, spoiled—utterly unacceptable to the owner.

What had happened? The owner moans and disclaims responsibility: "What more was I to do for my vineyard that I have not done in it?" (Isa. 5:4). The fault had to be in the vines.

Isaiah applies the parable to Israel, identifying the vines as the twelve tribes. From these vines God had expected justice and righteousness. But what was produced, especially in Judah, was oppression and bloodshed, cries for help from those who were oppressed (vs.7).

The lesson is clear. Fruit grows out of faith and faithfulness. Our good works, the expression of righteousness and justice through us, is the result of God's activity in us. "Bad fruit" is the result of our rejection of God, our arrogant understanding that we can make it on our own.

Keep the connection clear. There is no conflict between God's sovereignty and our human activity. We are saved *for* good work, though not *by* good works. Martin Luther's *The Shorter Catechism* puts it this way: "Sanctification is the work of God's free grace, whereby we are renewed in the whole [person] after the image of God, and are enabled more and more to die unto sin, and live unto righteousness."

REFLECTING AND RECORDING

Spend a few minutes reflecting on this truth: We are saved *for* good works, though not *by* good works.

How is this truth being reflected in your life?

DURING THE DAY

Observe people today. See how clearly you see in them the vital connection between the tree and its fruit.

"Every Tree That Does Not Bear Fruit Is Cut Down"

We cannot consider the Christian faith and life without giving some thought to judgment. There is no way to edit out the notion of judgment, either from the Bible or from life itself. Our decisions and actions have consequences.

I know a young man who wants desperately to be an investment banker. He has a master's degree in finance, but there is a big holdup. He may not make it. When he was nineteen, he was addicted to drugs, was indicted for theft and convicted as a felon. He has been drug-free for eight years, but the cloud is there and he waits anxiously to see what the judgment will be. Will he be licensed to buy and sell stocks and bonds?

I know a young woman who is happily married. She and her husband are two of the most dynamic Christians I know. The only dark cloud in their life is that they will never have children. As an eighteen-year-old, long before marriage, she became pregnant. Without a personal faith to guide her and without the support of a Christian community, she had an abortion. Something went wrong and now she is incapable of bearing children.

We could call to mind story after story. There is a law of judgment written into the fabric of life. What we do, what we believe, how we live in relationships, all have consequences. It has nothing to do with religion per se, it is simply how life is. But there is also an explicit Christian fact of judgment. It is the witness of scripture that God is the judge before whom persons and nations must and do stand in judgment.

> *Though the wicked sprout like grass and all evildoers flourish, they are doomed to destruction forever, but you, O LORD, are on high forever...The righteous flourish like the palm tree, and grow like a cedar in Lebanon. They are planted in the house of the LORD; they flourish in the courts of our God.*
> —Psalm 92:7-8, 12-13

> *Beware of false prophets, who come to you in sheep's clothing but inwardly are ravenous wolves. You will know them by their fruits. Are grapes gathered from thorns, or figs from thistles? In the same way, every good tree bears good fruit, but the bad tree bears bad fruit. A good tree cannot bear bad fruit, nor can a bad*

> *tree bear good fruit. Every tree that does not bear good fruit is
> cut down and thrown into the fire. Thus you will know them by
> their fruits.*
>
> —Matthew 7:15-20

This is an essential part of the biblical revelation. God created the world, called it good, and set before human beings the choice of good and evil. Life depends on that choice. Adam and Eve were cast out of the Garden of Eden because of their disobedience. Cain was made to wander on the face of the earth because he murdered his brother. The story of judgment goes on. Book after book in the Bible sounds a clarion note that there will be a day of judgment.

The psalmist painted the contrast between the grass which soon perishes and the palm tree and cedar tree which enjoy a long and fruitful life. The wicked are like grass; the godly are like the cedar and the palm, "like a tree planted by the rivers of water," bearing foliage and fruit (Psalm 1:3, KJV). The psalmist knows the secret of the fruit-bearing person; his source of life is to be found in the house of God, in the courts of God.

> *The Psalmist has not only frequented the house of God, he car-
> ries with him all the time what the house of God symbolizes: God
> is really with him, . . . he feels in his heart the forgiveness which
> flows from the altar; he has been cleansed by the water of the
> laver; the light of the golden candle-stick has fallen on him, and
> his prayers like incense have been presented to the throne of
> God; blood has been sprinkled for him on the mercy-seat and in
> the strength which comes from God's nearness (symbolized by
> the eating of the show-bread) he will not fear a hot drought from
> the desert. His supply of grace is perpetual, inexhaustible, and
> fresh every morning.*
>
> —John W. Sanderson

Jesus paints the judgment picture in even more vivid terms. Good trees bear good fruit; bad trees bear bad fruit. You will know them by their fruits. "Every tree that does not bear good fruit is cut down and thrown into the fire" (Matt. 7:19).

There is judgment. We must bear fruit. It is not enough simply to say, "Lord, Lord," we must do the will of our Father. Jesus made that scathingly clear in his picture of "the last judgment" (Matt. 25:31-46). The Son of Man will come with angels, and sit on the throne of his glory. He will offer the blessings of the kingdom to some, and others would be sent away "into the eternal fire prepared for the devil and his angels" (vs. 41). The basis on which we will be judged is our attitude and action toward others—the hungry, the thirsty, the stranger, the naked, the sick, the prisoner. "Just as you did it to the least of these who are members of my family, you did it to me" (vs. 40).

With this notion of inevitable judgment solidly in mind, let's look at a common designation we hear often: the carnal Christian. The Bible uses a number of terms to identify the carnal nature. A common one that we have looked at before is "flesh"—the way most translators render the Greek word *sarx*. Paul, the most ardent exponent of this idea, explains it this way: "For what the flesh desires is opposed to the Spirit, and what the Spirit desires is opposed to the flesh; for these are opposed to each other, to prevent you from doing what you want" (Gal. 5:17). He refers often to the "old nature" and to our "sinful nature."

The study of scriptures relating to this nature of our being reveals two basic facts. One, because of the Fall and sin—our fall and our sin—we are self-centered and rebellious, at enmity with God. Two, this aspect of our being is not immediately or completely eradicated by our conversion. The miracle of grace is not that we are accepted because we are without sin, but "while we still were sinners, Christ died for us" (Rom. 5:8). The power of the "flesh," our old nature, to operate and prevail in our lives is neutralized as we yield ourselves to the Lordship of Jesus Christ. "There is therefore now no condemnation for those who are in Christ Jesus. For the law of the Spirit of life in Christ Jesus has set you free from the law of sin and death" (Rom. 8:1-2).

Again, fruit is the issue. Pay attention to this word of judgment from John the Baptist:

> *But when he saw many Pharisees and Sadducees coming for baptism, he said to them, "You brood of vipers! Who warned you to flee from the wrath to come? Bear fruit worthy of repentance. Do not presume to say to yourselves, 'We have Abraham as our ancestor'; for I tell you, God is able from these stones to raise up children to Abraham. Even now the ax is lying at the root of the trees; every tree therefore that does not bear good fruit is cut down and thrown into the fire."*
>
> —Matthew 3:7-10

Note the phrase "bear fruit worthy of repentance." He is addressing this word to religious people, in fact, the most religious of his day—the Pharisees and Sadducees—those who defined and championed "the law." He tells the complacent Jews that spiritual identification and security did not lie in simply being law-keeping religious Jews, but in producing "good fruit." Fruit worthy of repentance grows out of a knowledge of our failure to be who God calls us to be, and an acknowledgment of the fact that without God and an utter dependence upon the grace of God, we are but chaff which will be separated from the wheat on the Day of Judgment. We are the fruitless tree that will be cut down and thrown into the fire.

REFLECTING AND RECORDING

Can you think of a person, such as the two I described—one "paying a price" for an abortion, the other whose chosen career may still be threatened by an addiction which he has overcome? Briefly tell the story.

Has a similar thing happened in your life? Are you "paying a price" for earlier habits, life-style issues, decisions? It is all in the past, but the result is still present. Describe the situation in a few sentences.

Spend a few minutes examining your thoughts and feelings about the fact of God's judgment.

Is there anything in your past that still "haunts" you, gives you uneasiness of conscience, fills you with shame and guilt?

Is it possible that you may not have yet repented and actually accepted the Lord's forgiveness for what is plaguing you? Examine yourself honestly; confess to the Lord, earnestly repent—be genuinely sorry—and receive Christ's forgiveness and healing. It doesn't matter what it is. If we repent, God promises to pardon and will take our sin from us "as far as the East is from the West."

DURING THE DAY

Stay vigilant in assessing your life today and in the following days. Try to locate specific occasions or expressions of walking in, being led by, or living by the Spirit.

DAY FIVE

The Singers of Life

We turn now to hope. Faith and hope are inextricably linked in the Christian way. Loren Eiseley, the anthropologist who writes some perceptive and challenging commentaries on life from his observation of nature, provides a dramatic picture suggestive of Christian hope. One day he leaned against a stump at the edge of a small glade and fell asleep:

> *When I awoke, dimly aware of some commotion and outcry in the clearing, the light was slanting down through the pines in such a way that the glade was lit like some vast cathedral. I could see the dust motes of wood pollen in the long shaft of light, and there on the extended branch sat an enormous raven with a red and squirming nestling in his beak. The sound that awoke me was the outraged cries of the nestling's parents, who flew helplessly in circles about the clearing. The sleek black monster was indifferent to them. He gulped, whetted his beak on the dead branch a moment and sat still. Up to that point the little tragedy had followed the usual pattern. But suddenly, out of all that area of woodland, a soft sound of complaint began to rise. Into the*

glade fluttered small birds of half a dozen varieties drawn by the anguished outcries of the tiny parents.

No one dared to attack the raven. But they cried there in some instinctive common misery. The bereaved and the unbereaved. The glade filled with their soft rustling and their cries. They fluttered as though to point their wings at the murderer. There was a dim intangible ethic he had violated, that they knew. He was a bird of death. And he, the murderer, the black bird at the heart of life, sat on there, glistening in the common light, formidable, unmoving, unperturbed, untouchable.

The sighing died. It was then I saw the judgment. It was the judgment of life against death. I will never see it again so forcefully presented. I will never hear it again in notes so tragically prolonged. For in the midst of protest, they forgot the violence. There, in that clearing, the crystal note of a song sparrow lifted hesitantly in the hush. And finally, after painful fluttering, another took the song, and then another, the song passing from one bird to another, doubtfully at first, as though some evil thing were being slowly forgotten. Till suddenly they took heart and sang from many throats joyously together as birds are known to sing. They sang because life is sweet and sunlight beautiful. They sang under the brooding shadow of the raven. In simple truth, they had forgotten the raven, for they were singers of life, and not of death.

—Eiseley, pp. 36–37

This is nature's witness to the truth of the Christian faith. Faith in Jesus Christ, His life, teaching, death, and resurrection, makes us "singers of life, not of death." As we have already pointed out, at the heart of faith is trust. We not only trust Christ, we trust God who gave the Son for our salvation, who raised him from the dead, and who has, even now, "raised us to newness of life." The resurrection of Christ is the sign of hope that all God's promises will be vindicated.

Let us hold fast the confession of our hope without wavering, for he who promised is faithful; and let us consider how to stir up one another to love and good works.

—Hebrew 10:23-24, RSV

This has special meaning in relation to our sorrow, disappointment, pain, and suffering. In the resurrected Christ, we know that the power of the "old age" is doomed and the "new creation" is already appearing. As Christians, we are called to make all of our life, and especially our suffering, an act of self-giving love, which is what it means to take up our cross and follow Jesus. The cross, which defines Jesus' life and which is to define ours, always carries with it the promise of resurrection. James S. Stewart puts the issue sharply:

It is one thing to preach the Cross as the last word of divine rev-
elation. It is quite another thing to preach it as the road travelled
once for all by One now known to be alive for ever.

—Stewart, p. 111

As persons in Christ, which is what we Christians are, we share in Christ's risen life. The divine energy which first took Jesus out of the grave is available to us—not only to raise us from death at our journey's end, but to empower us to grow up into "the full stature of Christ" now.

It's a matter of faith, and faith is a matter of trust, and trust gives us hope. We are singers of life.

REFLECTING AND RECORDING

Reinhold Niebuhr, one of the most influential theologians of the twentieth century, gave a meaning-packed summary of the theological virtues:

Nothing worth doing is completed in our lifetime; therefore, we
must be saved by hope. Nothing true or beautiful makes sense in
any immediate context of history; therefore, we must be saved by
faith. Nothing we do, however virtuous, can be accomplished
alone; therefore, we must be saved by love.

Spend some time pondering these statements. Is Niebuhr right? In what way is he right?

Look at your life and locate a time when hope was your sustaining source. Write a brief description of that experience.

DURING THE DAY

Look for signs of hope in your community, among people, in organizations and institutions. What seems to be the source of hope? Is it lasting?

DAY SIX

Agents of Hope, Enemies of Optimism

> *It is good to give thanks to the LORD, and to sing praises to Your name, O Most High; to declare Your lovingkindness in the morning, and Your faithfulness every night, on an instrument of ten strings, on the lute, and on the harp, with harmonious sound. For You, LORD, have made me glad through Your work; I will triumph in the works of Your hands. O LORD, how great are Your works! Your thoughts are very deep. A senseless man does not know, nor does a fool understood this. When the wicked spring up like grass, And when all the workers of iniquity flourish, It is that they may be destroyed forever. But You, LORD are high forevermore.*
>
> —Psalm 92:1-8, NKJV

We make a serious mistake when we identify optimism with hope. Though often confused, they are not the same. In fact, as Colin Morris has said:

> *Christians are, at one and the same time, agents of hope and enemies of optimism. It is utterly beyond me how anyone, Christian or not, can see substantial cause for optimism in this world. In essence, optimism is the brave but erroneous belief that our best efforts must produce proportionately good results. But they don't—and that I needn't bother to prove; history has saved me the trouble. I would certainly affirm the converse: the worst efforts of men can and do make the world even more of a living hell than it would otherwise be. Bitter personal experience, let alone a Biblical understanding of history, gives the lie to any philosophy of secular optimism. A warped world takes our*

brightest and best intentions and twists them into the material
of disappointment and failure....

There is something essentially morbid about optimism. The
optimist's personality is often attractive, but his soul is diseased.
It is insensitive to the power of evil. He believes either that evil is
illusory—if ignored, it will go away—or that it is a wasting asset
like many of the material elements which compose the earth.
Like coal or oil, its quantity of evil is finite and will slowly but
surely be consumed by the white fire of idealism or humanitar-
ian zeal."

—Morris, pp. 78–79

We can keep the distinction between optimism and hope when we accept the fact that progress and goodness are not inevitable. Society as a whole, if changed at all, is worse rather than better than fifty years ago. It's obvious on every hand the Christian God has been dethroned, and other gods are to be seen everywhere. When millions of people are dying from hunger around the world and in the United States, and books on dieting are instant best-sellers, can we be optimistic? In 1992 three abortions were performed in the United States every minute. In 1995 a total of 1.3 million abortions were performed in the United States, and two out of three of these for birth control and convenience. Can we now entertain the notion that the Reign of God has come near? When, in our nation, we are on the verge of making physician-assisted suicide legal, what can be said about humankind becoming Christlike? When the laws of the nation have given rights to racial minorities, but our racial prejudices have hardened, what is said about our love for one another?

We could go on. Optimism is not essential for kingdom reality. In fact, it is an enemy. But optimism is not hope. Hope is altogether something else, and hope is the essence of the Reign of God. Hope is the confidence that God is alive and sovereign. We trust that, in ways we may not understand, God is at work, and one day will establish God's kingdom. So, with the psalmist, we proclaim God's love in the morning and God's faithfulness at night (see Psalm 92: 2).

We will pursue this thought tomorrow as we consider the ethics of hope.

REFLECTING AND RECORDING

Spend some time pondering this statement: *Christians are, at one and the same time, agents of hope and enemies of optimism.* Do you agree? Without explanation, how might it be misleading?

Locate a personal experience when you were sustained by hope, but without optimism. Describe that experience.

DURING THE DAY

Sometime during the day talk with two people whom you consider "optimists." Question them about the source of their optimism. Is it grounded in a superficial understanding of human nature, or is it rooted in authentic Christian hope?

DAY SEVEN

Ethics of Hope

Our Father in heaven, hallowed be your name. Your kingdom come. Your will be done, on earth as it is in heaven. Give us this day our daily bread. And forgive us our debts, as we also have forgiven our debtors. And do not bring us to the time of trial, but rescue us from the evil one.

—Matthew 6:9-13

Christians the world over, in various words, pray the above prayer, adding, "For Thine is the kingdom, and the power, and the glory for ever and ever." We call it The Lord's Prayer. In this prayer we make the petition, "Thy kingdom come, Thy will be done, on earth as it is in heaven." It is obvious that this prayer is yet to be answered. Things are not as they should be; life is certainly not as God intended it to be.

Yesterday we considered the difference between secular optimism and Christian hope. The condition of the world offers no cause for optimism. The reality and power of God offers every reason for hope. Because the hard world gives no sign of hope, there is no excuse for Christians to sit back, fold their arms and do nothing except bewail their miserable fate.

If we believe and trust God enough to pray "Thy Kingdom come, Thy will be done," then we must order our lives and relationships, establish our priorities, and use our resources as though the Kingdom had come. Thus we approximate in this earthly order that which already exists in the heavenly realm. We practice what someone has designated the "ethics of hope."

> *We go to those in Rwanda and other places who are starving.*
> *We feed them and tell them a better day is coming.*
>
> *We go as servants to the oppressed on the Gaza Strip and other places.*
> *We minister to them in every way possible and explain to them*
> *that deliverance will one day come.*
>
> *We go to the lonely, the sick, the dying and tell them in words*
> *and deeds, by our presence, they are loved.*

Our presence and ministry will be signs, however limited, of hope. We will be witnesses to the coming Reign of God that we do not bring, but is the will and work of God. As Christians, we do not hunker down in retreat or wring our hands in despair, no matter what is going on in the world. We have only two legitimate positions—on our knees in prayer, saying, "Lord, have mercy on me, a sinner," or on our feet, standing erect, saying, "Here am I, Lord, send me." Despair paralyzes. Hope mobilizes. Christians have hope.

In his resurrection, Jesus Christ has conquered death and has given us a guarantee of life everlasting, and a kingdom that will know no end, a kingdom where nothing can separate us from the love of God in Christ Jesus (Rom. 8:38-39).

Everything that touches our fear and anxiety—from growing older to not having enough food, from the specter of random crime and violence to short tempers that fly when our comfort zone is invaded—has its roots in our fear of death, the ultimate enemy.

This death has a thousand faces. Because Jesus endured to the ultimate extent his undeserved death and because God raised Jesus, to live in the power of the resurrection and eternity under God's rule is to lose our fear of death, and to trust God to save us now and forever. This is Christian hope.

REFLECTING AND RECORDING

Pray the Lord's Prayer as you know it.

Concentrate for a few minutes on the petition "Thy Kingdom come." Think of those areas in your family and community where it is obvious that the kingdom has not come. Name those areas.

What "ethics of hope" might you practice in relation to these?

DURING THE DAY

Think of some situation or person to whom you might be a sign of hope today and act accordingly.

GROUP MEETING FOR WEEK FOUR

Introduction

John Wesley called on Christians to use all the "means of grace" available for their Christian walk, their growth in Christlikeness. Along with those means we normally think of—prayer, scripture, study, worship, Holy Communion—Wesley named Christian *conferencing*. By this, he meant intentional Christian conversation—talking about spiritual matters and sharing our Christian walk.

These group sessions provide practice in the art of Christian conferencing. As you share together in the "safe" setting of a group of mutually-committed persons, you are being equipped to share in less safe relationships. Keep this in mind as you share in this session and as you continue your weekly gatherings.

Sharing Together

1. You have finished four weeks of this workbook journey. Spend a few minutes talking about the experience in general terms. What is giving you difficulty? What is providing the most meaning?

2. Now spend ten to fifteen minutes discussing the "vital connection" which we considered on Day One of this week: faith and works. Be personal. Is your effort at "good works," being a person of virtue, an effort at *good works* to please God? Examine the assertion, "We are saved for good work, though not by good works."

3. Invite two or three persons to share their personal experiences of trusting Christ which they registered in the Reflecting and Recording period of Day Two, page 84. Reflect on what these experiences say about justification by grace through faith, and being saved for good works, though not by good works.

4. On Day Four, we considered the inevitable fact of judgment. Spend about ten minutes talking about the law of judgment written into the fabric of life. Perhaps some persons might share personal experiences that verify this. Distinguish between this life-judgment and God's judgment.

Consider how repentance relates to God's judgment, but does not alter some of the results of our actions.

5. Invite someone to read aloud to the group Neibuhr's work on page 93. Spend just a few minutes discussing in what way he is right.

6. Invite a couple of people to share their experience of hope as the sustaining strength of their life.

7. Spend about ten minutes talking about secular optimism as an enemy of Christian hope.

8. Discuss the ethics of hope concretely and personally. What are the areas in your family and community where it is obvious that the Kingdom has not yet come? How does Christian hope call you to respond?

Praying Together

Corporate prayer is one of the great blessings of the Christian community. Will you be a bit bolder now and experiment with the possibilities of corporate prayer by sharing more openly and intimately?

1. Let as many persons who will share a need in their life. These needs might include

- a need to trust Christ more;
- the pain of "paying the price" for something you have done in the past;
- an unwillingness to forgive someone who has done something for which you are suffering;

- a failure to invest yourself in love because you think the situation is hopeless.

2. Now join in corporate prayer with as many people as are willing to offer verbal prayers for those who have shared specific needs and/or concerns.

3. Sing a chorus or a verse of a hymn everyone knows, such as "Amazing Grace," "He Is Lord," or "Jesus Loves Me."

4. Pray together The Lord's Prayer.

Week Five

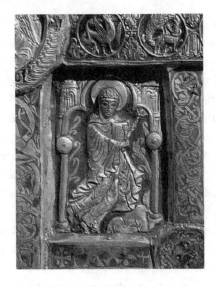

The Fruit of
the Spirit: Love

Works of the Flesh, Fruit of the Spirit

As indicated in the introduction and considered more fully last week, it is our conviction that any consideration of an explicitly Christian "moral" or "good" life must include the fruit of the Spirit named by Paul in Galatians 5:22-23: "But the fruit of the Spirit is love, joy, peace, longsuffering, kindness, goodness, faithfulness, gentleness, self-control. Against such there is no law" (NKJV).

We have dealt with the classic virtues: wisdom, courage, justice, and temperance, and last week we began to talk about the theological virtues. Paul named these at the close of his magnificent Hymn of Love, 1 Corinthians 13: "And now abide faith, hope, love, these three; but the greatest of these is love" (NKJV). We are adding to these what Paul called the *fruit of the Spirit*, the listing which he gave in Galatians 5:"

On Day Three of Week One, we stated that the literal meaning of the Greek word for virtue (*arete*) is power. The virtues in our lives are evidence of God's power of goodness at work within us.

We have also made the case more than once that while we are to discipline ourselves in practicing these virtues, their power lies in the fact that they are God-given rather than humanly achieved. That's the reason Paul calls them fruit of the Spirit. They are the result of the Spirit at work within us.

This week we look at love, which is one of the theological virtues, and also heads the list of the fruit of the Spirit. Before we look at a singular fruit of the Spirit, let's take a broad look at the setting in which Paul gives us this listing:

> *I say then: Walk in the Spirit, and you shall not fulfill the lust of the flesh. For the flesh lusts against the Spirit, and the Spirit against the flesh; and these are contrary to one another, so that you do not do the things that you wish. But if you are led by the Spirit, you are not under the law. Now the works of the flesh are evident, which are: adultery, fornication, uncleanness, lewdness, idolatry, sorcery, hatred, contentions, jealousies, outbursts of wrath, selfish ambitions, dissensions, heresies, envy, murders, drunkenness, revelries, and the like; of which I tell you beforehand, just as I also told you in time past, that those who practice such things will not inherit the kingdom of God. But the fruit of the Spirit is love, joy, peace, longsuffering, kindness, goodness, faithfulness, gentleness, self-control. Against such there is no law. And those who are Christ's have crucified the flesh with its passions and desires. If we live in the Spirit, let us also walk in the*

Spirit. Let us not become conceited, provoking one another, envy-
ing one another.

—Galatians 5:16-26, NKJV

Many of us may be familiar with Edward Sanford Martin's "My Name Is Legion."

Within my earthly temple there's a crowd;
There's one of us that's humble, one that's proud,
There's one that's broken-hearted for his sins,
There's one that unrepentant sits and grins;
There's one that loves his neighbor as himself
And one that cares for naught but fame and self.
For much corroding care I should be free
If I could once determine which is me.

Do you feel that way sometimes? We do. Don't we come all too frequently to those days when we are so befuddled and immobilized by the perplexity of our own human nature that we wonder if we can even call ourselves Christians? We're torn within. There's so little of Christ's peace and power in our life.

It is during those times that we appreciate the Apostle Paul so much. He could have written Martin's poem. In fact he said it as grippingly, maybe more so, as he dared to include in his letter to the Romans a conversation he had with himself. Few of us would risk being so honest and vulnerable, so visceral in expressing our perplexity and despair. Wrestling with himself—the life and death struggle between flesh and Spirit going on within, Paul concluded in Romans 7:19 and 24: "For the good that I would, I do not: but the evil which I would not, that I do. O wretched man that I am! Who shall deliver me from the body of this death?" (KJV).

We know the struggle, don't we? In the classical scriptural language of Paul, it is the internal war between Spirit and flesh.

We have considered this internal struggle on different days of our workbook journey, but it is such a crucial issue that we must revisit it often. It helps to get clarity about Paul's use of the terms *flesh* and *Spirit.*

For Paul, flesh is not a reference to our physical body. In his writing he used a different Greek word for flesh than he used for body. Nor did Paul equate flesh and sin. Paul was talking about two domains of power in which we live: the domain of the world, and the domain of Christ. To be sure, to live in the flesh is to live as a member of human society in a physical body. Yet Paul contrasts "walk-ing in the Spirit" and "living in the flesh" because our predicament is not that we live in a human body, but that we are in sin; that is, we live according to our sin-ful world (flesh), rather than according to the Spirit as a domain of power.

Paul is urging the Galatians to remember that as Christians they have received the Spirit, and they are to walk in the Spirit. The Spirit is the supreme energizing force in our lives.

For Paul, the Spirit is more than the manifestation of a supernatural power, more than the giver of dramatic gifts, more than an explosive force erupting in the believer now and then. The Spirit is the daily sustaining, inspiring, and guiding power of the Christian's life.

It is absolutely impossible to live within our own strength the kind of life Christ has called us to live. Is there anything more energy draining and disappointing than a vision without the power to live it? Is there anything more debilitating than to hear a call to do something or be something and yet be unable to respond? Such is not the case for the Christian. When we say, "I believe in the Holy Spirit," we affirm that we believe there is a living God who is able and willing to enter human life and change it. That's what Paul is telling us: When we walk in the Spirit, rather than live according to the flesh, there is an auxiliary power that is given us and this Spirit-power produces fruit—love, joy, peace, patience, goodness, faithfulness, kindness, generosity, gentleness, and self-control.

REFLECTING AND RECORDING

Paul lists what he calls the *evident* works of the flesh:

adultery	jealousies
fornication	outbursts of wrath
uncleanness	selfish ambitions
licentiousness	dissensions
idolatry	heresies
sorcery	envy
hatred	murders
contentions	drunkenness
revelries	

Look at the list above as you examine your own life. Put a check (✓) on the right side of any that you have experienced in the past month. Remember, this workbook is private; since no one will see it, be honest.

Now go back over the list and put a plus (+) on the right side of any with which you are tempted enough to take note of.

Now circle the one with which you have the most trouble.

Spend the balance of your time reflecting on whether your personal experience verifies Paul's picture of two *domains of power* in which we live: flesh and spirit.

DURING THE DAY

Examine the reactions you make to people and situations today. Register in your awareness any occasion when you had to resist the temptation to respond "according to the flesh."

DAY TWO

Love, a Cross-Style of Life

> *But the fruit of the Spirit is love, joy, peace, longsuffering, kind-*
> *ness, goodness, faithfulness, gentleness, self-control. Against such*
> *there is no law. And those who are Christ's have crucified the*
> *flesh with its passions and desires. If we live in the Spirit, let us*
> *also walk in the Spirit. Let us not become conceited, provoking*
> *one another, envying one another.*
>
> —Galatians 5:22-26, NKJV

When Paul named what has come to be called the theological virtues—faith, hope, and love—he said, "But the greatest of these is love." When he named the "fruit of the Spirit," he began with love. Who would question the centrality of love in the shape of the Christian life? The questions are:

What is the nature of this love?

How do we appropriate it?

How does it express itself in our lives?

To begin to answer these questions, we look to Jesus.

> *Let the same mind be in you that was in Christ Jesus, who,*
> *though he was in the form of God, did not regard equality with*
> *God as something to be exploited, but emptied himself, taking the*
> *form of a slave, being born in human likeness. And being found*
> *in human form, he humbled himself and became obedient to the*
> *point of death—even death on a cross.*
>
> —Philippians 2:5-8

Look at a story that will stimulate perspective: Roy L. Smith, a popular Methodist preacher and writer, grew up on the plains of Kansas when times were very hard. His father worked as a miller but never made more than a few dollars a week. Roy wanted more than anything to go to the little Methodist college in his hometown. But he knew it wasn't possible; his family simply didn't have the money. Yet, it happened. Somehow his parents were able to scrape up and save enough money to get him enrolled. Early in his college career, Roy was given a part in a debate that put him on stage. He wanted a new pair of shoes for the big day. Again, he didn't see how it was possible, but somehow, out of their meager income, his parents managed to buy some new shoes for their son.

Just before Roy went onstage, someone burst through the doors of the auditorium and shocked him with the news that his father had been hurt badly in an accident at the mill. He ran down the streets of that little town to the mill, but it was too late. His father had died.

After the funeral, Roy went to the mill to get his father's tools and the coveralls that he had been wearing at the time of the accident. Someone had thoughtfully folded up the bloody coveralls and then had placed his father's old shoes, bottom-side-up, in the tool box. When Roy opened it, the first thing he saw was his father's shoes. Those shoes had large holes in the soles. In that second, it all came flooding in. Roy realized that while he stood in his new shoes, his father had stood on the cold steel floor of that mill in shoes that didn't protect his feet. Pain and numbness captured Roy's heart.

That experience was a birth pang of new life for Roy Smith. He would never forget the love of his father. He knew that it was from that deep love that everything else flowed. He yielded his life to Christ and answered the call to preach and became a popular and powerful witness to the Christian faith. He said he never preached a sermon in which he didn't have a strong emphasis on the love of God.

That's a contemporary picture, though admittedly limited, of how it was with the Apostle Paul. He saw it clearly on the road to Damascus. He caught the vision, not of an earthly father in worn-out shoes on the cold steel floor of a mill, living in sacrificial love for his children, but in the gift of the Eternal Father of his son Jesus, who hung bare-hearted on a cross out of love for you and me. It was this love, the crucified love of Christ on the cross, that Paul was talking about: "in Christ God was reconciling the world to himself" (2 Cor. 5:19).

The above passage from Philippians is one of the most beautiful descriptions of Christ in scripture. It is also a description of Christian obedience and discipleship. It is the ultimate paradigm for love—a pattern for us to follow: "Let this mind be in you which was also in Christ Jesus" (Phil. 2:5, NKJV).

Christ's obedience to the point of death is offered to the Philippians (and to us) as a pattern for our own obedience. Just as Jesus obediently suffered, so the Philippians (and we) should stand firm in the gospel, even when it requires us to suffer (Phil. 1:27-30). Just as Jesus humbled himself and took upon himself the form of a slave, so the Philippians (and we) should become servants in love to others.

Whenever Paul talks about who Jesus was and what Jesus did, he always talks about the cross. The cross was the event in which God acted for the redemption of all humankind. It was also, for Paul, the paradigm for the obedience of all who are followers of Christ, a paradigm for the life of faith. When he wrote in Galatians 6:2, "Bear one anther's burdens, and in this way you will fulfill the law of Christ," Paul has taken the pattern of Christ's self-giving on the cross and made it the imperative for the Christian community to serve one another in love.

REFLECTING AND RECORDING

Jesus' willingly giving himself to death on the cross is the ultimate paradigm of love. If Jesus is our exemplar of love, then these phrases from Philippians 2 must also describe our love. Spend some time thinking about each phrase, testing your life by it: 1) "Did not regard equality with God as something to be exploited"; 2) "But emptied himself, taking the form of a slave . . . he humbled himself"; 3) "And became obedient to the point of death."

Now make some notes underneath each phrase, acknowledging your failure in following the pattern of Jesus—specific ways you fail—and how you must change for this pattern to be reflected in your life.

1. "Did not regard equality with God as something to be exploited"

2. "But emptied himself, taking the form of a slave . . . he humbled himself"

3. "And became obedient to the point of death"

Paul insisted over and over again that the Christian lifestyle is a cross-style. The cross is the definition of how the Christian is to love. His most descriptive word about Jesus is found in Philippians 2:5-8 quoted above. Notice how the passage begins, "Let this mind be in you that was in Christ Jesus" (vs. 5). Not only is this a description of who Jesus is, it is a call to us Christians. Spend the balance of your time pondering the question: How would I have to change to have the mind of Christ?

DURING THE DAY

As you move through the day, keep this picture of Jesus as the exemplar of love from Philippians 2 in mind. Call the picture to mind when you have to make a decision about some action or attitude you must take.

DAY THREE

What Kind of Service

Yesterday we focused on Philippians 2:5-8 as the ultimate paradigm of love. Go back and read that Philippians passage now.

We asked you yesterday to examine your life in relation to some of the descriptive phrases about Jesus in this passage. One of the phrases is "though he was in the form of God, did not regard equality with God as something to be exploited." It is not easy to identify with this action of Jesus because we do not see ourselves "in the form of God," or approaching the level of "equality with God." Yet, we need to press the issue of whether we do not, in fact, see our relationship to God as "something to be exploited." Do we use our relationship with God to enhance our image in the community? Do we pray only when we are pushed againt the wall or when we want something?

If someone who knew you intimately wrote a biography of you, what would she write about most? What are the activities that demand most of your attention? Who are the persons to whom you give most of your time? What really excites you and gives you joy and meaning?

When the author specifically described your Christian life, what would she write about?

- what you believed and how tenaciously you held to certain doctrines?
- your faithfulness in church attendance?
- the positions you held in the church organization?

- your prayer life?
- how effectively you witnessed to the faith?

How much would she write about your lifestyle as a servant? And how would she describe how you served? What would she say about whether you saw your relationship to God as "something to be exploited?"

The core issue is love. Love as the fruit of the Spirit must be love after the style of Jesus. As we have seen, this love is that of one who "emptied himself, taking the form of a slave . . . humbled himself and became obedient to the point of death." Not many of us want to be servants like that, do we? Examine the way we serve. We choose when, where, how, and whom we will serve. We stay in charge. When we serve in the style of Jesus, we give up the right to be in charge. We empty ourselves (become vulnerable). We humble ourselves (give up control). We become obedient (sacrificially offer what we have and who we are). When we cease seeing our relationship to Christ as something "to be exploited," then we lose our fear of being stepped on, or manipulated, or taken advantage of. Love becomes the power for action and attitude that gives us "the mind of Christ," thus we look like him in the pattern of our lives.

REFLECTING AND RECORDING

Go back in your mind to the notion of someone writing a biography of you. What about your life might your biographer write that would make you happy? Don't be modest. Make a few notes here.

What do your wish your biographer could say about you, but your life is "not there yet?" Make some notes.

Close your time in reflection by focusing on the need to get your life in harmony with the pattern of Jesus.

DURING THE DAY

Keep a close eye on your attitudes and actions today. Check your temptation to serve how, when, where, and whom you please, rather than being an obedient servant after the style of Christ.

DAY FOUR

They Will Know We Are Christians by Our Love

We sing it to a lilting tune, adaptable to most any musical instrument, but made popular in more contemporary worship with the use of guitar and keyboard. "They will know we are Christians by our love, by our love, yes, they'll know we are Christians by our love."

The question is, Do they? Do the people around us know we are Christians by our love? A lot is being written these days about the "cultural war." On every hand, this workbook included, the Church seeks to make a convincing apologetic for Christian values in society, to stage a powerful beachhead against moral relativism and secular materialism.

Our militancy on behalf of values is dulled, at least a bit—or should be—when we consider the "cultural war" with which Jesus had to deal. John Ortberg has put it into perspective:

> *It is interesting that the people who held the "right" values were the ones least responsive to Jesus' message and most likely to receive his reprimands. His message was received with the greatest eagerness by those who came down on the wrong side of all the values issues—the prostitutes, the tax collectors, the religious half-breeds....*
>
> *The ironic result of their [the Pharisees'] "rightness" in belief and practice was that they became unable to love—did not want the sick healed on the Sabbath, did not want an adulterous woman to be forgiven, did not want sinners to share fel-*

*lowship with the righteous. They came to see people they were
called to love as "the enemy."*

—Ortberg, p.25

The truth we need to remember is that we can be right—and yet act wrongly. Being right and knowing it often produces loveless, calloused sermons. We can be so intent on preserving our rightness, our values, that we fail to love. When being right and being on the right side becomes our driving passion, it is easy to forget the heart of the gospel. Jesus said that the heart of the law is to love God with your entire being and to love your neighbor as yourself (Matt. 22:37-40). And note the dramatic way Paul put it:

> *Though I speak with the tongues of men and of angels, but, have not love, I have become as sounding brass or a clanging cymbal. And though I have the gift of prophecy, and understand all mysteries and all knowledge, and though I have all faith, so that I could remove mountains, but have not love, I am nothing. And though I bestow all my goods to feed the poor, and though I give my body to be burned, but have not love, it profits me nothing.*
>
> —1 Corinthians, 13:1-3, NKJV

Our primary task as Christians is not to make a rational apologetic for Christian values, but to participate in and witness to the gospel, which has love as its core. We need an *experiential* apologetic far more than we need an intellectual one. Jesus didn't say, "All persons will know you are my disciples if you present a convincing argument or promote my agenda." He did say, "All will know you are my disciples, if you love one another." As we considered yesterday, we demonstrate "the mind of Christ" by loving and serving as he did.

REFLECTING AND RECORDING

Having been involved in this workbook journey for four weeks now, spend a few minutes reflecting on the struggle involved in "being good," in allowing virtue to grow in your life.

On Day Seven of Week One, we asked you to reflect on two questions: Do you genuinely want to be good? Are you seeking moral sincerity and integrity? Reflect on those questions again. Are there changes in the way you would respond now?

When has your life of virtue, or your seeking to be good kept you from loving? Recall times when you have been good, you have "kept the law" and remained righteous, but failed to love?

Is your intellectual case for the Christian more convincing than your experiential witness or how you relate to others in love?

If you have passed over the last two exercises quickly, ask yourself why? Do you have difficulty examining how you love?

Write a prayer confessing your failure to love.

DURING THE DAY

As you move through the day note how many more opportunities you have to act the Christian life than to talk about it.

Grace, All Grace!

For when we were still without strength, in due time Christ died for the ungodly. For scarcely for a righteous man will one die; yet perhaps for a good man someone would even dare to die. But God demonstrates His own love toward us, in that while we were still sinners, Christ died for us. Much more then, having now been justified by His blood, we shall be saved from wrath through Him. For if when we were enemies we were reconciled to God through the death of His Son, much more, having been reconciled, we shall be saved by His life. And not only that, but we also rejoice in God through our Lord Jesus Christ, through whom we have now received the reconciliation.

—Romans 5:6-11, NKJV

In the book *In The Grip of Grace*, Max Lucado tells a story that exemplifies grace.

Once a monk and his apprentice traveled from the abbey to a nearby village. The two parted at the city gates, agreeing to meet the morning after completing their tasks. According to plan, they met and began the long walk back to the abbey. The monk noticed that the younger man was unusally quiet. He asked him if anything was wrong. "What business is it of yours?" came the terse response.

Now the monk was sure his brother was troubled, but he said nothing. The distance between the two began to increase. The apprentice walked slowly, as if to separate himself from his teacher. When the abbey came in sight, the monk stopped at the gate and waited on the student. "Tell me, my son. What troubles your soul?"

The boy started to react again, but when he saw the warmth in his master's eyes, his heart began to melt. "I have sinned greatly," he sobbed. Last night I slept with a woman and abandoned my vows. I am not worthy to enter the abbey at your side."

The teacher put his arm around the student and said, "We will enter the abbey together. And we will enter the cathedral together. And together we will confess your sin. No one but God will know which of the two of us fell.

—Lucado, pp. 91-92

There is a sense in which this story describes what Christ has done for us. "While we were still weak. . . . while we were yet sinners. . . . Christ died for us . . . While we were enemies, we were reconciled to God through the death of his Son." In our Christian vocabulary, the word for it is *grace*. Story after story in scripture paints the picture.

Hosea takes back his whoring wife, in love and forgiveness, as a parable of who God is. Grace, all grace!

A son rebels against his father, leaving home to squander his inheritance in a foreign land. Yet his father waits patiently for his return; and when he finally arrives, throws a grand celebration of welcome. Grace, all grace!

Jesus refuses to allow a woman taken in the act of adultery to be stoned, because none of us is without sin and God forgives. "Neither do I condemn thee, go and sin no more." Grace, all grace!

A woman of the street "crashes a party" where Jesus is the guest. The host would have thrown her out, but Jesus reminds him that the woman was expressing love because she knew forgiveness and pity. The host didn't know that love and forgiveness yet. Grace, all grace!

Grace is undeserved, unearned, unmerited acceptance. The grace of God is God's unconditional love for us. Though we may never love in God's way, that is the standard. Max Lucado has given us a litany of experiences followed by piercing questions that give us the right perspective:

> *Your friend broke his promises? Your boss didn't keep her word? I'm sorry, but before you take action, answer this question: How did God react when you broke your promises to him?*
>
> *You've been lied to? It hurts to be deceived. But before you double your fists, think: How did God respond when you lied to him?*
>
> *You've been neglected? Forgotten? Left behind? Rejection hurts. But before you get even, get honest with yourself. Have you ever neglected God? Have you always been attentive to his will? None of us have. How did he react when you neglected him?*
>
> —Lucado, pp. 155–156

REFLECTING AND RECORDING

Recall an experience when you were loved undeservedly and unconditionally. What had you done or failed to do? Who expressed the love? Why did you feel it was undeserved? How did the one who loved you show it? Record that experience here.

Have you ever experienced the love Christ in a way that comes close in fact and feeling to the experience you just described? Make some notes about that experience here.

If you haven't experienced the love of Christ as you have experienced the unconditional love of another, can you believe that Christ loves you even more unconditionally and extravagantly? Spend your closing time thinking about Christ's love for you. "For when we were still without strength, in due time Christ died for [us]" (Rom. 5:6, NKJV).

DURING THE DAY

George Matheson wrote a hymn of commitment to the love, light, and joy of Christ. The first stanza of that hymn is printed on page 191. Cut it out, and put it in a place where you will see it and have access to it during the coming days—in your pocket or purse, on the dashboard of your car, in your date book, on the bathroom mirror or refrigerator door. If you know the tune sing it, or simply read it,-but make it your prayer today and during the coming days.

> O Love that wilt not let me go,
> I rest my weary soul in thee;
> I give thee back the life I owe,
> That in thine ocean depths its flow
> May richer, fuller be.

DAY SIX

No Escape from Love's Demands

Love suffers long and is kind; love does not envy; love does not parade itself, is not puffed up; does not behave rudely; does not seek its own, is not provoked, thinks no evil; does not rejoice in iniquity, but rejoices in the truth; bears all things, believes all things, hopes all things, endures all things. Love never fails.

—1 Corinthians 13:4-8, NKJV

Recently our daughter and sister, Kerry, and her husband, Jason, adopted a baby. In the midst of this moving experience of love and hope and excitement, we thought about stories that we've heard and read concerning adoption. In the best case scenarios the adoptive parents and children bond to create a family unit. In less than ideal situations the family is thrown into chaos. One such example is a couple who was in the process of adpoting a teenage boy. The boy was unruly and disobedient. Family members and friends urged the couple not to adopt, comforting them by saying that the boy was not their real son anyway. But the couple displayed uncondtional love and wanted to keep their commitment to the boy who needed a mother and father. They continued with the adoptive process.

We can argue about this couple's approach but not about their love. We may debate the right ways of expressing love, but we must be careful that we don't excuse ourselves from its demands.

There is also this less dramatic, but equally important issue: Love does not blind us to the faults of others, but prevents us from paying too much attention to those faults. François Fénelon challenged us in this way:

> *Charity does not demand of us that we should not see the faults of others; we must in that case shut our eyes. But it commands us to avoid attention unnecessarily to them, and that we be not blind to the good, while we are so clear-sighted to the evil that exists. We must remember too God's continual kindness to the most worthless creature, and think how many causes we have to think ill of ourselves and finally we must consider that charity embraces the very lowest human being. It acknowledges that in the sight of God the contempt that we indulge for others has in its very nature a harshness and arrogance opposed to the spirit of Jesus Christ. The true Christian is not insensible to what is contemptible; but he bears with it.*
>
> —Fénelon, Day 60

REFLECTING AND RECORDING

In your own relationships, right now, who is the person you are finding most difficult to love? Name that person: _____

Paul gave some specific attributes of love in 1 Cornithians 13:

Suffers long	Thinks no evil (not resentful)
Kind	Does not rejoice in wrong
Not envious	Rejoices in truth
Does not parade it (not boastful)	Bears all things
Not puffed up (not arrogant)	Believes all things
Not rude	Hopes all things
Does not insist on its own way	Endures all things
Not provoked (not irritable)	

Go through the list and place a check beside those attributes of love which you are not expressing toward the person named above.

Spend some time thinking about how you might begin to incorporate the attributes you checked into your love for the person named above.

DURING THE DAY

Continue using the hymn-prayer, "O Love That Wilt Not Let Me Go."

DAY SEVEN

Love and Forgiveness

On Day Five of this week, we considered grace, the unconditional, unmerited, undeserved, unearnable love of God. The primary expression of grace is acceptance and forgiveness. We can measure the way the fruit of love is growing in our lives by our willingness and readiness to accept and forgive.

Is there a more desperate need? The sense of shame and guilt cripples us and keeps us in bondage to that which brings the shame and guilt. It drives us into isolation and compulsion, keeps us dependent on our addictions. Though the alcoholic hates herself, she continues to drink. The overeating person, though burdened with shame, continues to binge. The lying man, shamefaced and guilt stricken, lives in dread and terror of being caught again, but continues to lie. "If they only had the willpower," we think, and they often feel. But Jesus knew, and counselors have learned, that love that accepts and forgives is the only power that can penetrate the human heart and bring change. The person needing acceptance and freedom must love herself, yes! but love must come from another as well. In fact, it is almost always true: We come to love ourselves when we experience the love of Christ. And it is likewise almost always true: We experience the love of Christ when we are loved by another.

Watching Jesus as he moves through the Gospels, we discover, as Margaret Gramatky Alter has reminded us, that he acts on two basic beliefs about human nature: the universal need of forgiveness and the abiding presence of an interested and compassionate God. The radical nature of Jesus' relationship is that his forgiveness is not contingent upon our actions or attitudes. He doesn't ask for an apology—and, shockingly, he doesn't ask for repentance. Alter says, "It is as if the forgiveness precedes repentance; forgiveness itself creates safety for individuals to recognize how terribly alienated they are, how needy, how empty."

This encounter of Jesus tells the story.

> *Then the scribes and Pharisees brought to Him a woman caught in adultery. And when they had set her in the midst, they said to Him, "Teacher, this woman was caught in adultery, in the very act. Now Moses, in the law, commanded us that such should be stoned. But what do You say?" This they said, testing Him, that they might have something of which to accuse Him. But Jesus stooped down and wrote on the ground with His finger, as though He did not hear. So when they continued asking Him, He raised Himself up and said to them, "He who is without sin among you, let him throw a stone at her first." And again He stooped down and wrote on the ground. Then those who heard it, being convicted by their conscience, went out one by one, beginning with the oldest even to the last. And Jesus was left alone, and the woman standing in the midst. When Jesus had raised Himself up and saw no one but the woman, He said to her, "Woman, where are those accusers of yours? Has no one condemned you?" She said, "No one, Lord." And Jesus said to her, "Neither do I condemn you; go and sin no more."*
>
> —John 8:3-11, NKJV

Commenting on the story, Alter says:

> *[Jesus] insists on the universal human need for forgiveness. He returns again to his writing, and in the confrontative silence [the accusers] leave. He has opened a healing possibility to them. Now that they too acknowledge their alienation, their sin, they also can receive forgiveness and rejoin the community.*
>
> *As Jesus is left alone with the woman, we see again the unusual quality of his forgiveness; personal, tender, understated, an unconditional positive valuing. Jesus not only offers to relieve her burden and her shame, but he offers her an additional protection, the right to refuse sexual overtures and therefore the chance to end the abuse. "Go on your way, and from now on do not sin again," he says, empowering her to say no, to set boundaries.*
>
> —Alter, p. 30

Here is the pattern for love as the fruit of the Spirit to grow in our lives. It is more radically demanding than anything we can anticipate. The result of it is more radically transforming than we can imagine. When we love enough to accept and forgive, we participate with Christ in breaking the power of canceled sins and in setting captives free.

REFLECTING AND RECORDING

Yesterday you were asked to name the person who you are finding most difficult to love. Think about that person now. Does the reason it is difficult for you to love him or her have something to do with forgiveness? Do you need forgivness from that person or do you need to forgive him or her? Think about it for a moment.

Other than the person you have been thinking about, name a person from whom you need to seek forgiveness. Then name a person you need to forgive.

You can initiate forgiveness from the person you have wronged or hurt; with persons who have wronged or hurt you the case is different. They may not acknowledge their need to be forgiven and seek your forgiveness. Spend some time thinking about how you can handle each case.

Write a prayer requesting God's help in dealing with the two persons named above.

DURING THE DAY

Take some specific steps in making real forgiveness with the persons mentioned above.

GROUP MEETING FOR WEEK FIVE

Introduction

Paul advised the Philippians to "let your conversation be as it becometh the gospel of Christ" (Phil. 1:27, KJV). The Elizabethan word for *life* as used in this King James Version is *conversation*. Most of us have yet to see the dynamic potential of the conversation which takes place in an intentional group such as this. Life is found in communion with God and also in conversation with others.

Speaking and listening with this sort of deep meaning which communicates life is not easy. This week our emphasis has been on love. All of us have deep experiences of love: being loved, failing to love, not loving ourselves, deep experiences not easy to talk about. Therefore, listening and responding to what we hear is very important. To really hear another person helps him or her to think clearly and gain perspective. It may contribute to the healing process. To listen, then, is an act of love. When we listen in a way that makes a difference, we surrender ourselves to the other person, saying, "I will hear what you have to say and will receive you as I receive your words." When we speak in a way that makes a difference, we speak for the sake of others; thus we are contributing to the wholeness process.

Sharing Together

1. Spend six or eight minutes discussing Paul's distinction between spirit and flesh.

2. Now spend eight to ten minutes talking about this assertion: "The cross is the definition of how the Christian is to love."

3. Invite two or three persons to name and describe a person they know who is practicing a cross-style of love.

4. In the Reflecting and Recording period of Day Three you were asked, "What about your life might your biographer write that would make you happy?" Ask two or three persons to share their response?

5. You were also asked, "What do you wish your biographer could say about you, but your life is 'not there yet'?" Share responses to this question?

6. Spend ten to fifteen minutes talking about how we can be right and yet act wrongly. Give examples without violating persons. Be personal. Has your life of virtue, or your seeking to be good, kept you from loving? Is your intellectual case for the Christian faith more convincing than your experiential witness—how you relate to others in love?

7. Invite persons to share an experience of unconditional love.

8. Talk about how these experiences just shared speak about grace. Can persons witness to experiencing the love of Christ in the same way?

PRAYING TOGETHER

These weekly sharing sessions are actually "prayer meetings." When we are together in Jesus' name, Jesus is there. We listen to others in love. We share, believing that we can be honest because we are loved and are gathered in the name and the spirit of Jesus. So there is a sense in which, throughout your sharing, you have already been corporately praying. As already indicated however, there is power in a community on a common journey verbalizing thoughts and feelings to God in the presence of fellow pilgrims. Let that be the case now.

1.   Let the leader call each person's name, pausing briefly after each name for some person in the group to offer a brief verbal prayer, focused on what that person has shared. It should be as simple as "Lord, thank you for helping Jane to have confidence that she is forgiven," or "Loving God, give John the sense of your direction as he has shared what he feels is missing in his life." (Leader, remember to call your own name.)

2.   When all names have been called and all persons prayed for, sit in silence for two minutes; be open to the strength of love that is ours in community. Enjoy being linked with persons who are mutually concerned.

Week Six

Joy and Peace

The Words and the Tune

Mark Twain's wife did her best to censor the more picturesque flights of her husband's language. One morning he cut himself shaving and cursed long and loud. When he stopped, his wife tried to shame him by repeating to him verbatim all the profanities that he had just uttered. Twain heard her out and then remarked, "You have the words, my dear, but I'm afraid you'll never master the tune."

Good for her! Yet her situation is suggestive of the state of many Christians which is not good. We know the words, but we need to master the tune. As Christians we are the recipients of the Holy Spirit. A new kind of power, a new kind of action, a new kind of life is now possible. But it is not automatic.

It's a great day in our lives when we discover that the Holy Spirit and the indwelling Christ are one. It is the witness of Scripture and is clear in the words of Jesus himself.

> *If you love me, you will keep my commandments. And I will ask the Father, and he will give you another Advocate, to be with you forever. This is the Spirit of truth, whom the world cannot receive, because it neither sees him nor knows him. You know him because he abides with you, and he will be in you. I will not leave you orphaned; I am coming to you. In a little while the world will no longer see me, but you will see me; because I live, you also will live. On that day you will know that I am in my Father, and you in me, and I in you.*
>
> —John 14:15-20

The setting for this teaching helps us understand and appropriate what Jesus is saying. Jesus is preparing the disciples for his death. He tells them that he is going away; he is going to prepare a place for them but will come again "and will take you to myself, so that where I am, there you may be also" (John 14:3) Thomas questions the whole affair: "We don't know where you're going, and we don't know the way" (14:5, AP) Jesus defines himself as he makes the claim, "I am the way, and the truth, and the life. No one comes to the Father except through me" (vs. 6).

Philip, still puzzled, presses earnestly: "Lord, show us the Father, and we will be satisfied" (vs. 8). Now comes Jesus' word about his oneness with the Father.

Jesus said to him, "Have I been with you all this time, Philip, and you still do not know me? Whoever has seen me has seen the Father. How can you say, 'Show us the Father'? Do you not believe that I am in the Father and the Father is in me? The words that I say to you I do not speak on my own; but the Father who dwells in me does his works."

—John 14:9-10

Following this revealing exchange, Jesus continues to talk about his death and resurrection, promising that he would not leave us alone but would send an Advocate, a Comforter, one to be with us forever. Now here is the key. When Jesus promised the gift of the Holy Spirit, he immediately identified himself with the Spirit. "I will not leave you orphaned; I am coming to you" (vs. 18).

The words and the tune come together. Jesus is the revelation of God and the personification of the Holy Spirit. The Spirit who gave us faith to accept Christ as Savior is the spirit within us as the indwelling Christ. He is with us now to give us faith and the will to yield ourselves to Jesus as Lord. He is with us now to produce the "fruit of the Spirit"—the sign of Christ alive within us.

The words and the tune come together. The tune is joy. In *Orthodoxy*, G. K. Chesterton said, "Joy . . . is the gigantic secret of the Christian" (page 298). Here it is in a person described by Mary Lou Carney in *Spiritual Harvest*.

Ina folded her silk dresses into the trunk. Their bright ribbons and delicate laces felt strangely foreign to her fingertips. She read, again, the telegram that had arrived yesterday. "Father is ill. Please come home." She blinked back tears as her ears filled with the remembered applause of appreciative audiences.

Ina Ogdon was a woman of both talent and personality. Her voice, her stage presence, her illustrious start—all pointed to a great future in the theater. Then came that life-changing, dream-shattering telegram.

So home she went to look after her invalid father. Ina's stage was now her kitchen floor and the confines of the sickroom. Her audience was reduced to family. . . . And her song? Did it shrivel into the bitterness of her soul? Hardly! She determined to let her light shine, even without the glare of stage lights. She not only learned the lesson of unconditional joy, but also taught it, by contagion, to those around her.

Then, in 1913, Ina Ogdon put her philosophy into poetic form by writing the gospel song "Brighten the Corner Where You Are." It's chorus admonished:

Brighten the corner where you are.
Brighten the corner where you are.
Someone far from harbor
You may guide to the bar.
Brighten the corner where you are!

First sung at a great meeting in Syracuse, New York, the song met with instant and wide acceptance. The girl who left the public pleasure of performing for the private task of service soon found her tune, and her name, on the lips of people everywhere.

—Carney, pp. 36-37

Joy is the Christian's gigantic secret.

REFLECTING AND RECORDING

Spend a few minutes reflecting on the fact that the "fruit of the Spirit" is the sign that Christ is alive within us.

Below is a listing of the "fruits of the Spirit." Put a check (✓) over the ones most evident in your life.

Love Joy Peace Patience Kindness

Goodness Faithfulness Gentleness Self-control

Spend a few minutes reflecting on how this fruit has grown in your life. What did you do to cultivate it? How is the fruit an expression of Christ alive within you?

Offer a prayer of thanksgiving for the fruit that is growing within, and pray that other fruit will begin to grow.

DURING THE DAY

As you observe people today, seek to detect which ones have the gigantic secret of the Christian life—joy. Also, pay close attention to your attitudes and actions today. See if you can see signs of any "fruit of the Spirit" other than what you checked above.

DAY TWO

Cloning Joy—Don't We Wish?

My Father is glorified by this, that you bear much fruit and become my disciples. As the Father has loved me, so I have loved you; abide in my love. If you keep my commandments, you will abide in my love, just as I have kept my Father's commandments and abide in his love. I have said these things to you so that my joy may be in you, and that your joy may be complete.

—John 15:8-11

In early 1997, the world was shocked with news coming out of Scotland. The Scottish cell biologists, Dr. Ian Wilmut and Dr. Keith Campbell had created the previous year the first clone of an adult mammal . . . a sheep which he named "Dolly."

Not just the scientific world, but the general public was astir. What did this mean? What were the possibilities for human cloning? What were the moral, ethical, and spiritual implications? When we hold in our hands the capacity to replicate adult human beings, the implications are mind-boggling and heart-stopping.

Ellen Goodman concluded a newspaper column entitled "We may learn a moral lesson from ewe clones" with a sobering, sensible word:

> *If I am allowed to find any good news in the Valley of the Dollys, maybe the cloning controversy will help us to get a grip on the current argument about nature vs. nurture.*
>
> *Of late, it seems that our fascination with the biological basis of everything has led to a belief that DNA is destiny. In a perverse way, Dolly may force us to remember that people are not just conceived, we are raised. We are the products of our environments as well as our genes. The point is that we can clone biological potential, but not real people. At seven months, Dolly is all done.*
>
> —Goodman, p.13A

There is no possibility of cloning joy. It is the unique experience of each person. Yet, no matter who we are and where we are, joy can be ours. It is the promise of Jesus. It is not a matter of cloning, but of abiding . . . that is, abiding in Christ. The passage with which we began today comes from the fifteenth chapter of John, which begins with Jesus' revealing metaphor of the vine and the branches. Jesus tells us who God is and who he is in relation to God: "I am the vine and my Father is the vinegrower" (vs. 1). Then Jesus tells us who he is and who we are in relation to him: "I am the vine, you are the branches" (vs. 5). The vinegrower provides life for the vine and the vine provides life for the branches, and they are all connected. So Jesus calls us to abide in him as the branches abide in the vine. If we do that, we will abide in Jesus' love and joy will be ours. "I have said these things to you so that my joy may be in you, and that your joy may be complete" (vs. 11).

Our joy is dependent upon our abiding in Christ. Self-centeredness is the barrier to our abiding in him. Our basic problem is that we have dislodged God from the center of our being; self-interest, self-serving, self-worship have taken God's place.

Back to the cloning issue. Bioethicists describe self-cloning as the most narcissistic act imaginable. Is it stretching the thought stream too far to suggest that the possibility of that narcissistic act is the extreme to which we are going as we keep self enthroned? We were created by God with personalities that can only operate properly when fed by God's love. When we seek to run our own life on our terms, dominated by self-interest, we separate ourselves from the stream of love and joy that flows only from God. We position ourselves with the big "I" dominating the canvas of our world. That is what sin is and that's what separates us from God.

REFLECTING AND RECORDING

Below is a listing of the fruits of the Spirit. As you did yesterday, put a check mark over the ones most evident in your life.

Love Joy Peace Patience Kindness

Goodness Faithfulness Patience Self-control

Look at the list again. Circle the two "fruits" *least evident* in your life.

Reflect for a few minutes on this question: Is the absence of these "fruits of the Spirit" in my life connected with my failure to abide in Christ?

Spend the balance of your time answering these two questions:
To what degree am I actually abiding in Christ?

To what degree do I really want to abide in Christ?

DURING THE DAY

Psalm 92:4 says, "For you make me glad by your deeds, O LORD; I sing for joy at the works of your hands" (NIV). This verse is printed on page 191. Cut it out and carry it with you for the next few days. Read it often and memorize it. Use it to call to mind that the works of God and our relationship to Christ is our source of joy.

DAY THREE

Sources of Joy—The Outcome of Faith, The Salvation of Your Souls

Blessed be the God and Father of our Lord Jesus Christ! By his great mercy he has given us a new birth into a living hope through the resurrection of Jesus Christ from the dead, and into an inheritance that is imperishable, undefiled, and unfading, kept in heaven for you, who are being protected by the power of God through faith for a salvation ready to be revealed in the last time. In this you rejoice, even if now for a little while you have had to suffer various trials, so that the genuineness of your faith—being more precious than gold that, though perishable, is tested by fire—may be found to result in praise and glory and honor when Jesus Christ is revealed. Although you have not seen him, you love him; and even though you do not see him now, you believe in him and rejoice with an indescribable and glorious joy, for you are receiving the outcome of your faith, the salvation of your souls.

—1 Peter 1:3-9

A handwritten letter came from The Broadmoore, in Colorado Springs, Colorado, one of America's premier hotels. The writer lived in Indiana. Maybe he was on a business trip or vacation. Whatever the case, he was in a reflective mood and wanted to share with me, even though we had never met. He identified himself and told his story.

> *Dear Dr. Dunnam,*
>
> *A little more than two years ago, out of sheer desperation, I began a spiritual journey that has transformed my life. Some of your work, especially* The Workbook of Living Prayer *and* The Workbook of Intercessory Prayer, *have been vital guideposts along that journey.*
>
> *My life was lost to alcohol and I was on the verge of losing my family, joy, money, and even my life. After a series of unsuccessful suicide attempts, God intervened through a number of agencies including AA and a rehabilitation center. As a result, I came to know God, then Jesus, and finally, the Holy Spirit—not overnight, but slowly, surely.*
>
> *I am enormously grateful to [God] for restoring my life and returning my family, health, joy, and showing me a way to live I never thought possible."*

What caused a person like this, a stranger, to take the time to share his joy with one he had never met? His was the "indescribable and glorious joy" Peter talked about. He was full of joy that he had to share because he was "receiving the outcome of [his] faith, the salvation of [his] soul" (vs. 9).

The primary source of our joy is the fact of our salvation. Too few of us reflect enough on this fact. This may be one of the reasons our joy is not "full." If we don't know that joy of salvation, it may be that we have not dealt deeply enough with our sin. There is a connection, even a parallel, between our sorrow for sin and our joy in the Holy Spirit.

In *A Diary of Readings* by John Baille, Blaise Pascal puts it in perspective: "The knowledge of God without that of our wretchedness creates pride. The knowledge of our wretchedness without that of God creates despair. The knowledge of Jesus Christ is the middle way, because in Him we find both God and our wretchedness" (Day 37).

There is a story in Luke's Gospel (chapter 7) about a woman "who was a sinner" crashing a dinner party where Simon, a wealthy Pharisee, was entertaining Jesus. It was a shocking interruption. She stood behind Jesus, who was reclining on the floor cushions around the table, and began to weep. Her tears gushed forth uncontrollably—so much so that she began to bathe Jesus' feet with her tears and dry them with her hair. It was an outrageous display in the eyes of Simon and the others. This woman of the street kept kissing Jesus' feet and anointing them with costly ointment.

Simon thought to himself, "If this man were a prophet, he would have known who and what kind of woman this is who is touching him—that she is a sinner" (vs. 39). It was quite the opposite. Jesus did know and so he confronted Simon.

> *Then turning toward the woman, he said to Simon, "Do you see this woman? I entered your house; you gave me no water for my feet, but she has bathed my feet with her tears and dried them with her hair. You gave me no kiss, but from the time I came in she has not stopped kissing my feet. You did not anoint my head with oil, but she has anointed my feet with ointment. Therefore, I tell you, her sins, which were many, have been forgiven; hence she has shown great love. But the one to whom little is forgiven, loves little."*
>
> —Luke 7:44-47

This woman was full of joy and abandoned all reserve. She took the initiative in seeking Jesus out in a place where she was not invited or welcome. With the boldness of one who knew the depth of her sin and the extravagant extent of Jesus' forgiveness, she poured out her love and gratitude.

There is a relationship, even a parallel, between our sorrow for our sin and our joy in the Holy Spirit.

REFLECTING AND RECORDING

When was the last time you shared with another person the joy of your salvation? Make notes here:

When:

With whom:

Spend a few minutes reflecting on these questions:
What kind of feelings did you experience in sharing your joy?
How did the person(s) with whom you shared respond?

Now reflect on these questions:
Is your salvation real enough to give you joy?
If so, why do you not share that joy with others more often?

DURING THE DAY

Look for an occasion today to share with another the joy that is yours because of your relationship to Jesus Christ. Continue to remind yourself by reading and possibly memorizing Psalm 92:4.

DAY FOUR

The Source of Joy: All Our Needs Will Be Supplied

Rejoice in the Lord always; again I will say, Rejoice. Let your gentleness be known to everyone. The Lord is near. Do not worry about anything, but in everything by prayer and supplication with thanksgiving let your requests be made known to God. And the peace of God, which surpasses all understanding, will guard your hearts and your minds in Christ Jesus.

—Philippians 4:4-7

Paul was in prison when he wrote his letter to the Philippians, yet this is one of his most remarkable contributions to us Christians. From prison, and nearing the end of his life, he wrote an appealing and a convincing argument for the Christian faith. It is Paul's most joy-filled letter. He calls on the Philippians to rejoice—not just to rejoice in one act of praise and thanksgiving, but to rejoice always.

The last two verses of his letter form the capstone and give the reason why joy is not only possible but is the logical response to the experience that is ours.

And my God will fully satisfy every need of yours according to his riches in glory in Christ Jesus. To our God and Father be glory forever and ever. Amen.

—Philippians 4:19-20

It's a bold affirmation: Our God will supply our every need "according to his riches in glory in Christ Jesus." One difference between happiness and joy is that happiness is tied to circumstances—what is going on around us. Joy is much deeper—it is not dependent on circumstances but on commitment and trust.

A big enemy of joy is self-pity. The antidote to self-pity is the confidence that God will supply our every need. To the degree that we lack that confidence, to that degree our joy will be limited.

Do you remember the story of Elijah in the Hebrew Scripture? He was overcome with self-pity when he began to think that God no longer pitied him. It happened when he heard that Jezebel had sent her soldiers to kill him (1 Kings 19:1-2). How quickly he had forgotten. God had intervened with direct and supernatural care by responding to his request that it not rain (1 Kings 17:1), feeding him through the ravens for an entire year (1 Kings 17:6), providing the support of a widow who hid him from his enemies (1 Kings 17:9), demonstrating faithfulness by sending fire to incinerate the altar when all the prophets of Baal couldn't get even a whimper from their god (1 Kings 18:38).

How quickly he forgot. So when Jezebel came after him, he gave in to self-pity. When immediate success and visible result did not come in his ministry, he wallowed deep in despondency: "It is enough; now, O LORD, take away my life, for I am no better than my ancestors" (1 Kings 19:4). How quickly we forget!

Elijah discovered, as we need to discover, that God does not always work in the ways we want God to. That doesn't mean God isn't working. Our joy is not in the way God works, or whether God works as we would desire and design—but *that* God works. For Elijah, God was not in the earthquake, wind, and fire, but in the still small voice.

REFLECTING AND RECORDING

Recall and record here an occasion when you knew God supplied your need. Write enough about the experience to remember the things that happened—what was going on in your life? What were your needs? How were those needs met? How did you feel and respond?

Are you struggling now with particular issues and needs, wondering why God doesn't help or intervene? You have prayed, but no answers seem to be forthcoming. Does your experience recorded above give you any clues about how you should respond to what is going on now?

Spend time affirming or seeking to claim the confidence expressed in this statement: *Our joy is not in the way God works but in the fact that God works.*

DURING THE DAY

Philippians 4:19-20 is printed on page 191. Cut it out, put it someplace where you can see it often during the day. Read it; claim the promise of it; memorize it so you can take it in your heart beyond this week.

DAY FIVE

Joy and Peace: Obedience Versus Duty

> *It is good to give thanks to the Lord, and to sing praises to Your name, O Most high; to declare Your lovingkindness in the morning, and Your faithfulness every night, on an instrument of ten strings, on the lute, and on the harp, with harmonious sound. For You, Lord, have made me glad through Your work; I will triumph in the works of Your hands. O Lord, how great are Your works! Your thoughts are very deep. A senseless man does not know, nor does a fool understand this. When the wicked spring up like grass, and when all the workers of iniquity flourish, it is that they may be destroyed forever. But You, Lord, are on high forevermore.*
> —Psalm 92:1-8, NKJV

The fruit of the Spirit are not isolated from each other; they overlap in meaning and expression. Some have special connections. Joy and peace go together. Neither is dependent upon circumstance. Both are by-products of obedience.

We need to stay aware of the fact that obedience and duty are not the same. We can be obedient without being preoccupied with duty. As joy is dependent upon abiding in Christ's love, so peace is dependent upon keeping our hearts and minds in Christ Jesus. Philippians 4:7 says, "And the peace of God, which surpasses all understanding, will guard your hearts and minds in Christ Jesus."

As the source of our joy is the fact of our salvation and the confidence that all our needs will be met, likewise our peace.

In his book *How to Live the Christian Life*, Selwyn Hughes tells of a preacher friend's encounter with the receptionist at a doctor's office. During the preacher's appointment with the doctor, he invited the receptionist to visit his church. He was stunned at her response. She said that when she saw so many of his church members waiting for their weekly supply of sedatives at the doctor's office on Monday morning, she really wondered what the church had to offer.

There were tears in the minister's eyes as he told Hughes the story, concluding, "Selwyn, it hurt so much because it was true." Reflecting on that experience, Hughes wrote:

> *If as Christians we claim to have abundant life, how does it happen that so many of us give so little evidence that this life is superior? We say that God is our Father and is quietly arranging all things to work to our good, yet we fly into a panic at the first approach of trouble. We claim Christ is Lord of our lives, yet when someone tramples on our rights we show by our actions who is really in command. We talk piously about peace, but when tragedy strikes, our peace goes into pieces. We preach forgiveness, but let someone injure us and see what happens.*
>
> —Hughes, pp. 14-15

The gap must be closed—the gap between what we profess and how we live. If, as we are contending, peace is the result of our acceptance of God's forgiveness in our lives, then we must keep that awareness alive, and we must practice forgiveness in all our relationships.

A friend shared with us this story. It was a matter of a disputed family will. The misunderstanding had bitterly estranged two sisters. The one who told the story confessed that her resentment darkened through the passing years and something beautiful died within. She was not only hurting her sister, she was injuring herself. Then on a Sunday, words of scripture in the worship liturgy took hold of her mind and heart: "For if you forgive others their trespasses, your heavenly Father will also forgive you; but if you do not forgive others, neither will your Father forgive your trespasses" (Matt. 6:14-15).

That afternoon she wrote a letter to her sister, a letter that breathed love, forgiveness, and reconciliation. She said, "When I dropped that letter into the mailbox, it was like a thousand 'alleluias' singing inside me. The world was beautiful again and I felt alive for the first time in years."

Peace and joy!

REFLECTING AND RECORDING

Who is the most peace-filled person you know? Name that person here.

As you know and have observed this person, what is the source of his/her peace? Make some notes.

Comparing yourself to this person, what is missing from your life, perhaps robbing you of peace? Make some notes.

Spend the balance of your time reflecting on this statement: Peace is dependent upon keeping our hearts and minds in Christ Jesus.

DURING THE DAY

Have you memorized Psalm 92:4? Do you have Philippians 4:19-20 in an available place to remind you of the vital truth that God will supply your needs in Christ Jesus? Immerse yourself daily in the claims and promises of these two passages.

DAY SIX

Peace: God's Presence
Despite the Circumstances

*On that day this song will be sung in the land of Judah: We have
a strong city; he sets up victory like walls and bulwarks. Open the*

gates, so that the righteous nation that keeps faith may enter in. Those of steadfast mind you keep in peace—in peace because they trust in you. Trust in the Lord forever, for in the LORD GOD you have an everlasting rock.

—Isaiah 26:1-4

The King James Version is a more familiar rendering of one of these verses. "Thou wilt keep him in perfect peace, whose mind is stayed on thee" (vs. 3). Peace is the product of the certainty of God's presence despite the circumstances. We have seen it as you have—and we may have experienced it:

- a person walking through the darkest valley of the shadow of death, yet radiating peace;
- a person living in horrendous circumstances that would drive a lesser soul to madness, yet moving through the clamor and confusion with quiet strength;
- another person being pulled in ten different directions—demanding work, sick wife, rebellious teenager. You wonder how he keeps from "flying to pieces," and then you discover why. You know he is being kept in peace because his mind is stayed on God.

I have a friend, a Methodist minister's wife, whose life is the most powerful witness I know of the peace that is the product of the certainty of God's presence despite the circumstances.

On New Year's Day, 1991, she and her ten-year-old daughter were headed home from celebrating the Christmas holidays with friends. She missed a turn and decided to take the next road, though it was not familiar to her. She topped a hill, to be greeted by a stop sign. She was going too fast to stop and went through the intersection and under the trailer of an eighteen-wheeler. Kari, the daughter, survived with minor lacerations and a mild concussion, but Roberta's spinal cord was injured and she was paralyzed from the neck down. There were broken ribs and a punctured lung. In the first week, she had three surgeries. In the beginning, she could only move her eyes.

The doctors told her husband that she would be better off dead; that if she lived, she would be bedridden, ventilator-dependent, and a vegetable. Telling me the story, she said, "The doctors told Earl (her husband) that he was too young to be saddled with an invalid wife and even offered some 'solutions.' But Earl chose life for me."

That was seven years ago. These years have been full of pain and struggle, hospitalization, and surgery after surgery. In a wheelchair and wearing a neck brace, she has now come to the place where she wears a splint on her right wrist, which enables her to use a push-button telephone, a computer, and feed herself.

When I saw a newspaper article about her activity, her speaking in church, and ministering in all sorts of imaginative ways, I wrote her a letter. She responded:

"My family is like any other family. We shop, go to movies, eat out, and take vacations. I'm still a quadriplegic. But by God's grace I'm also a pastor's wife, a mother, a registered nurse (inactive), a Certified Lay Speaker in our church, a Sunday school teacher, and an active member of the United Methodist Women. I continue to pray for physical healing, but I'm also aware of the great spiritual healing God has done in me and through me. His hand has been in my life throughout this journey. I know because I hold on to it and 'walk' with [God] every day."

REFLECTING AND RECORDING

Recall an experience in your life when despite circumstances you felt forsaken, alone, and abandoned—an illness, the death of a loved one, failure, loss of friendship or job. Record that experience in enough detail to get it fresh from memory.

Looking back on that experience, did you feel God's presence? How was God's presence experienced? Even though, then, you may not have felt and acknowledged God's presence, are there signs, in retrospect, that God was there—present and working? Spend time reflecting in that experience and the statement: Peace is the product of the certainty of God's presence despite the circumstances.

DURING THE DAY

Look for at least one peace-filled person today and ask them the source of their peace.

Knowing and Doing the Will of God

If you love Me, keep My commandments. And I will pray the Father, and He will give you another Helper, that He may abide with you forever—the Spirit of truth, whom the world cannot receive, because it neither sees Him nor knows Him; but you know Him, for He dwells with you and will be in you. I will not leave you orphans; I will come to you. A little while longer and the world will see Me no more, but you will see Me. Because I live, you will live also. . . . These things I have spoken to you while being present with you. But the Helper, the Holy Spirit, whom the Father will send in My name, He will teach you all things, and bring to your remembrance all things that I said to you. Peace I leave with you, My peace I give to you; not as the world gives do I give to you. Let not your heart be troubled, neither let it be afraid.

—John 14:15-19, 25-27, NKJV

There is no ongoing peace apart from keeping our mind stayed on Jesus.

We have spent our adult lives studying scripture, reading theology, writing sermons, preparing for worship, praying, seeking spiritually to lead congregations, caring for persons in need, and in the process receiving a lot of love and affirmation. Yet, there are times when we feel an absence of peace. A subtle franticness sets in and we become uneasy, uncertain, unproductive. We lose our sense of centeredness; sometimes a cloud of depression will hover over us. Sometimes this gloom and absence of peace is short-lived. Sometimes it's for a day, even a week.

The time is determined by how long it takes us to realize we have taken our eyes off Jesus. Our minds are not stayed on Christ. When we discover what priority has replaced Christ as the priority in our lives, then through prayer and commitment, we recover peace.

This is the first way to cultivate the certainty of God's presence, and thus receive the by-product of peace—keeping our minds stayed on Jesus.

In his book *Brother to a Dragonfly*, Will D. Campbell tells the story of one who transparently kept her mind stayed on Jesus.

And about Mrs. Tilly a little Methodist woman from Atlanta, who never weighed more than a hundred pounds in her life, who looked about eight years younger than God, joined forces with a group of forty thousand women in the thirties and forties in what they called the Association of Southern Women for the Prevention of Lynching. She was then active in advocating the desegregation of public schools and got a lot of obscene phone calls, calling her everything but the gentle woman she was. She had an engineer hook her telephone to a phonograph and when someone called her late at night the answer they heard was some deep-throated baritone singing The Lord's Prayer. The calls soon stopped.

—Campbell, p. 137

What imagination! But also what confidence in the Lord! No wonder Mrs. Tilly knew peace. She kept her mind stayed on Jesus.

Then there is a second realization. The Christian's peace is the companion to knowing and doing God's will. If we have been given marching orders in a particular area or relationship of our lives and have refused to follow, then we cannot know peace. If we pray, "Lord, what do you want me to do? Where do you want me to go? How do you want me to act?" and the Lord responds with direction that we consciously refuse to follow, we will not know peace. Faithful obedience is the environment essential for the fruit of peace.

It sounds presumptuous, but we have to give God "elbow room" in our lives. We have to make room and be willing to allow God to move in our lives as God pleases. However intimately we may know God, we never know God well enough to predict when and how God is going to act and what God is going to demand. Obedience must be our ready response.

I saw this stance of obedience and thus a peace that passes all understanding in the life of my friends Abel and Freida Hendricks. Abel, now retired, was a Methodist preacher in South Africa. He fought the battle against apartheid and stood with the poor and oppressed at great cost. I remember an occasion when he had been imprisoned by the government for his courageous opposition to oppression. I had a telephone conversation with him the day after his release. I was unaware, but later learned, that he was on the verge of nervous collapse; he had suffered so much physically and emotionally. He was very emotional, as we talked on the phone, even crying at times. But his words were strong and confident: "We're going to be all right. They can put us in prison; they can close our schools; they can continue to deny human rights and try to reduce us to animals. But they cannot take away our peace and joy in Christ."

Where is the secret of Abel and Freida's joy and peace? Keeping their minds stayed on Christ and knowing and doing the will of God.

REFLECTING AND RECORDING

Looking back on this week's reflection on joy and peace, spend time looking at your life in relation to the following questions. Do not move from one to the other until you have explored where you are now in relation to the fruit of joy and peace in your life. Does your life reflect the Christian's gigantic secret—joy?

If joy is dependent upon abiding in Christ, are you exercising the disciplines necessary to keep your relationship with Christ alive?

Do you rehearse in your mind enough and share with others your salvation story often to keep the experiences of God's grace which keeps your joy alive?

Do you concentrate too much on being happy which is dependent on circumstances rather than on joy which flows from our relationship to Christ?

Would those who know you say you are peace-filled?

Are you resisiting some call, failing to respond to what you know is God's will?

DURING THE DAY

Claim the promise and live in the confidence that God will keep in perfect peace those "whose mind is stayed on Thee."

GROUP MEETING WEEK SIX

Introduction

You are drawing to the close of this workbook venture. You have only two more planned group meetings. Your group may want to discuss the future. Would the group like to stay together for a longer term? Are there resources (books, tapes, periodicals) that the group would wish to use corporately? If you are a part of the same church, is there some way you might share the experience you have had with others? Test the group to see if they would like to discuss future possibilities.

Being a part of a group requires responsible participation. Some of us, in a group setting, feel the temptation to "play it safe" and not risk being honest and vulnerable. This is even true when we share about such positive issues as joy and peace.

Energy is another issue. Listening and speaking demands physical as well as emotional energy. So the temptation is to hold back, to be only half-present, not to invest the attention and focus essential for full participation. We urge you to withstand these temptations. These sharing sessions are very important. Don't underestimate the value of each person's contribution.

Sharing Together

1. Begin your time together by the leader offering an opening prayer or calling on someone else (consulted ahead of time) to do so. Then sing a chorus or a couple of verses of a hymn everyone knows.

2. The group has been together long enough for everyone to have a degree of trust and comfort. Turn to the Reflecting and Recording period on Day One, page 126. Ask each person to look at the "fruits of the Spirit" they checked as the ones most evident in their life. Let each person in the group name one "fruit" she checked and share briefly how this fruit has grown in her life and what she did to cultivate it. Don't think it prideful to share in this fashion.

3. All of our sharing should be punctuated with particular focused prayer. Ask someone to offer a brief prayer of thanksgiving for how the fruit growing in persons' lives is an expression of Christ alive and at work in their group and the world.

4. In the Reflecting and Recording period of Day Two, you were asked to check the "fruits of the Spirit" least evident in your life. Spend four or five minutes discussing how the absence of these "fruits of the Spirit" may be connected with our failure to abide in Christ.

5. Ask someone to read the quote from Blaise Pascal on Day Three, page 131. Spend four or five minutes discussing this assertion but also focus on how in Christ we realize our sinfulness.

6. Invite one or two persons to share an experience of sharing with another "the joy of their salvation."

7. Spend five to eight minutes talking about our sources of joy and peace being the fact of our salvation and the confidence that all our needs will be met.

8. Ask any persons who are willing to share any lack of peace they have, and what may be robbing them of that peace.

9. If persons do share, then after the sharing spend a minute or two in silent prayer on behalf of these persons.

10. Spend the balance of your time reading the questions guiding the

Reflecting and Recording for Day Seven. Discuss each of these questions as a group.

PRAYING TOGETHER

1. Ask if there are persons who are struggling with particular issues and needs, wondering why God doesn't help or intervene. Would they be willing to share about their situations that the group can pray for them? If so, when the sharing is done, spend a minute or two with everyone praying silently, then ask one person to offer a verbal prayer on behalf of the ones who have shared.

2. Spontaneous conversational prayer is a creative and guiding source in our corporate life. Close the time together by inviting as many as will to offer brief prayers growing out of their sharing tonight. Before you begin this, ask if anyone in the group has specific prayer requests, other than where you have already focused, especially areas where joy and peace may be missing.

When as many as wish to have prayed, close by inviting all to pray together The Lord's Prayer.

Week Seven

Patience

Kindness

Goodness

Patient Long-suffering

Our friend, Norman Neaves, a pastor in Oklahoma City, told a wonderful story in a sermon about a first-grade teacher who was having an unusually difficult day. It had rained that day and the children could not go out for recess. As the day wore on, the kids got more and more restless and very hyperactive. The teacher could hardly wait for the bell to ring at 3 o'clock.

About 2:45, she looked out and saw it was still raining, so she decided to start getting the kids ready for their dismissal. She sorted out their boots and their rain-coats and started helping get them on. Finally they were all ready to go with the exception of one little boy whose boots were just too small for his feet. There were no zippers and no snaps, and it took every last ounce of strength she had to get them on.

When at last she had them on, she straightened up with a sigh of relief. But do you know what the little boy said? He looked down at his feet for a moment and then said, "Teacher, you know what? These boots ain't mine!"

She didn't know whether to laugh or cry, but being the good teacher she was, she smiled bravely and started taking them off. And they were even harder to get off than they were to put on! She yanked and she tugged and she tugged and she yanked. Finally the boots came off. And you'll never guess what the little boy said. He smiled at his teacher and said, "They ain't my boots, but they're my sister's and I've got to wear them!"

It happens daily: Our patience is tried.

The Greek word is *makrothymise* and is translated "patience" and "forbearance" as well as "long-suffering."

> *The great church father and preacher Chrysostom said that it is the grace of the man who could revenge himself and who does not.*
>
> *The word is used generally as patience in regard to people, not to things or events. Certainly we have no difficulty thinking . . . that patience is another expression of love. In the great Hymn of Love (1 Cor. 13), Paul used the word to illuminate the nature of love: "Love is patient and kind."*
> —Dunnam, *The Communicator's Commentary, p. 117*

To grasp the meaning of patience as a fruit of the Spirit, we best begin by thinking of the patience of God with us. God suffers long, bears with us in all our sinning and rebellion, all our apathy and unconcern. God does not draw back when we spurn God's love.

The prophet Micah provides a marvelous picture of this patient, long-suffering God:

> *Who is a God like You, pardoning iniquity and passing over the transgression of the remnant of His heritage? He does not retain His anger forever, because He delights in mercy. He will again have compassion on us, and will subdue our iniquities. You will cast all our sins into the depths of the sea.*
>
> —Micah 7:18-19, NKJV

This is who God is, and Jesus reveals this patient, long-suffering God as the Shepherd who never gives up on a lost sheep, as a Father who waits and prays and prays and waits with outstretched hands and heart to receive the prodigal son back home.

REFLECTING AND RECORDING

What kind of situations "try" your patience most? Name two or three.

Why do these situations get to you? Is it a time issue? Is it a matter of control—you are not in complete control? Are feelings of threat involved? Spend time asking yourself why you become impatient in these situations.

Among the persons with whom you regularly associate, who are the ones who most often try your patience? Name two or three.

Spend some time thinking about why these persons test your patience. Is it a matter of control? Do you feel disrespect? Do you feel used?

DURING THE DAY

Take note of those times you lose patience today. Ask yourself, "Why is this making me impatient?"

DAY TWO

Love Is Patient and Kind

Though I speak with the tongues of men and of angels, but have not love, I have become as sounding brass or a clanging cymbal. And though I have the gift of prophecy, and understand all mysteries and all knowledge, and though I have all faith, so that I could remove mountains, but have not love, I am nothing. And though I bestow all my goods to feed the poor, and though I give my body to be burned, but have not love, it profits me nothing. Love suffers long and is kind; love does not envy; love does not parade itself, is not puffed up; does not behave rudely, does not seek its own, is not provoked, thinks no evil; does not rejoice in iniquity, but rejoices in the truth; bears all things, believes all things, hopes all things, endures all things.

—1 Corinthians 13:1-7, NKJV

Some Bible scholars believe that love is the one fruit of the Spirit, and joy, peace, patience, kindness, goodness, faithfulness, gentleness, and self-control are expressions of love. Whether or not this is strictly the case in Paul's understanding, it is doubtful if any fruit of the Spirit can grow in our life without love.

The patient long-suffering of God which we considered yesterday is certainly an expression of love.

In the great Hymn of Love (1 Corinthians 13), Paul used this word to illuminate the nature of love: "Love suffers long and is kind" (NKJV), or "Love is patient and love is kind." We often use this hymn of love in wedding ceremonies, for our contention is that the love which sustains a marriage is decision love—a love that practices patient long-suffering. We don't know any place where patient long-suffering is needed more than in the family—especially the marriage relationship.

When we marry a couple, we try to point out to them that what they are doing goes against the advice given by the culture in which we live. That advice is that if we're going to find happiness, then we've got to think only of ourselves. We're bombarded by self-centeredness—especially through advertising. If you want to find yourself, think of yourself. But the marriage vows say something else. In the marriage vows, we focus entirely on the other person. Love and care and fidelity to another person are not dependent on reciprocation. When you get married, you vow to give yourself unqualifiedly to another human being. That's a scary thing. It's really risking your life. The charge to the couple in the United Methodist marriage ritual reads like this: "Be well assured that if these solemn vows are kept inviolate as God's Word demands, and if steadfastly you endeavor to do the will of your heavenly Father, God will bless your marriage, . . . and will establish your home in peace." Do you see what that is saying? Blessings in marriage are by-products of giving ourself to our spouse. If we try to get those blessings in any other way, we will lose them. But if we give ourselves, we will find them.

Not only is patient long-suffering a saving quality in our marriage relationship, but how we need it as parents. How we need it in relation to aging parents—to keep on caring for those who have cared so long for us, or even to care for those who may not have cared for us. And we can't will this quality. It grows out of Christ's patience with us.

I don't agree with everything Ed Wheat says in his book *Love Life*, but I do believe in one strong point he makes about the negative role that even the possibility of divorce has upon a marriage relationship.

> *If you're trying to build a love relationship in your marriage, or if you're trying to work out problems in your marriage, even admitting the faintest possibility of divorce will affect your efforts adversely. Retaining the idea of divorce in your emotional vocabulary—even as a last-ditch option—will hinder the total effort you would otherwise pour into your marriage. . . . Keeping divorce as an escape clause indicates a flaw in your commitment to each other.*
>
> —Wheat, p. 38

Is that stating it too harshly? Well, think about it. Think about it in terms of love being patient and kind. Think about it in terms of the harvest of the Spirit in our life-patient long-suffering.

REFLECTING AND RECORDING

Focus on your family. If you are not presently living in a "family" situation, focus on the most intimate circle in which you move from week to week. Who are the persons who most often "get on your nerves" and try your patience? You may have named them in the Reflecting and Recording yesterday. List them here.

What role does selfishness play in what these persons do to try you? Think about it for a minute or two.

What role does selfishness play in making you impatient?

Read again Ed Wheat's word about divorce. Spend a few minutes examining your response to his statement: "Keeping divorce as an escape clause indicates a flaw in your commitment to each other."

Who are the persons in your life to whom you most need to express patient long-suffering? Name them.

Close your time praying for these persons you just named, and for yourself in relation to them.

DURING THE DAY

When you find yourself growing impatient today, remind yourself that the mark of a Christian is to be "patient and kind."

DAY THREE

Always in a Hurry

President Franklin D. Roosevelt and Prime Minister Winston Churchill were at the Yalta Conference with Joseph Stalin in 1945, trying to settle issues between nations following World War II. When Roosevelt said that he hoped that the conference would only last five or six days, Churchill responded, "I do not see any way of realizing our hopes about world organization in five or six days. Even the Almighty took seven."

One of our biggest problems is that we are always in a hurry. Ours is a fast-food, quick-fix, instant-replay culture. I could not have imagined, even five years ago, that I would be typing this manuscript on a computer and that I would be able to print copy instantly and preserve the copy on my computer to edit it as many times as I wished—and that has been many. Yet I found myself, just this morning, being irritated at the time it took to get the computer into the program I needed to begin this work on patience. That reminded me of a story of a man who prayed earnestly one morning for grace to overcome his besetting sin of impatience. A little later he missed his train by half a minute and spent an hour stamping up and down the station platform in furious vexation. Five minutes before the next train arrived, he suddenly realized that his prayer had been answered. He had been given an hour to practice the virtue of patience but had missed the opportunity and wasted the hour fuming.

The fruit of the Spirit, especially patience, cannot grow if we are always in a hurry. This fruit of the Spirit, Christian patience, is dependent upon our belief in a Sovereign God who is in control, who is at work in the world, and who will not forget any one of us. The psalmist sang about this:

> *I will praise You, O LORD, among the peoples, and I will sing praises to You among the nations. For Your mercy is great above the heavens, and Your truth reaches to the clouds.*
> —Psalm 108:3-4, NKJV

> *You are my rock and my fortress; therefore, for Your name's sake, lead me and guide me. Pull me out of the net which they have secretly laid for me, for You are my strength. Into Your hand I commit my spirit; You have redeemed me, O LORD God of truth.*
> —Psalm 31:3-5, NKJV

But not only in the Psalms, the witness is throughout the Bible: Our sovereign God is in control. God is at work in the world and will not forget any one of us. The prophet Isaiah put it this way, in one of the most haunting words in the Old Testament's record of God speaking of his people:

> *Can a woman forget her nursing child, and not have compassion on the son of her womb? Surely they may forget, yet I will not forget you. See, I have inscribed you on the palms of my hands.*
>
> —Isaiah 49:15-16, NKJV

We demonstrate our impatience more glaringly and most irreverently when we question God's timetable. How often and in how many ways does it happen? We expect God to act now. When we do not perceive signs of God's acting, we give up looking for God's activity in our life; even specific answers to prayer go unnoticed.

We also show the limitation of our patience when we are impatient with another person's weaknesses. This is one of our most glaring failures. We are quick to see the "speck" in another's eye and disregard the "beam" in ours. An antidote for this is to constantly remind ourselves of God's patience with us. Psalm 92 reminds us that it is good "to declare [God's] steadfast love in the morning" (vs. 2). If we keep reminding ourselves that God is committed to us, that our welfare is so close to God's heart and that God will not withhold or even modify one single promise, then we can show patience with another person's weakness. If God is patient with us, constant in lovingkindness, we certainly owe the same to others.

Another issue: When we are in a hurry, we can't pray. Prayer demands time, attention, silence, waiting. When we are in a hurry, we miss much of the beauty and meaning of life. In "Infirmity" the poet Theodore Roethke talks about seeing in a different way: "the deep eye sees the shimmer on the stone." If we are in a hurry we miss that . . . not only the shimmer on the stone, but also the glimmer on the grass, the yellow-breasted finch, first violets of spring, the beauty of the weeds, the dancing shadows of wind-motioned pines.

Roethke makes another suggestive statement. In "What Can I Tell My Bones," he says, "I recover my tenderness by long looking." Impatience mitigates against tenderness because there can be no long looking if we are always in a hurry.

REFLECTING AND RECORDING

Have there been occasions in the past few months when you were impatient with God? Name such an occasion and make some notes as to how your impatience expressed itself.

Write the name the one person with whom you have been most impatient because of his/her weakness. Think about how God has sought, or is seeking, to deal with that person.

How do you think God would want you to change in relation to the person you have named?

Spend a few minutes examining your prayer life. How much time are you spending in prayer? Do you have difficulty giving God your focused attention, even in specific times of prayer? Is your lack of patience adversely affecting your prayer life?

Test yourself now. See if you can spend three minutes in silence, thinking only about God.

DURING THE DAY

Move through this day with the "deep eye." Practice "long looking."

DAY FOUR

Kindness—Giving Others Strength and Power to Go On

Come to Me, all you who labor and are heavy laden, and I will give you rest. Take My yoke upon you and learn from Me, for I am gentle and lowly in heart, and you will find rest for your souls. For My yoke is easy and My burden is light.
—Matthew 11:28-30, NKJV

The word in this passage that describes Jesus' yoke as "easy" is the Greek word *chrestos*. It is the same word from which kindness as a fruit of the Spirit comes. It is sometimes translated gentleness.

> *Only slight shades of meaning differentiate these words. This is illustrated in the fact that the KJV uses the word* gentleness *at this point in the listing while the RSV and the NKJV use* kindness. *Then later when the NKJV uses* meekness *the RSV and the NKJV use* gentleness. *The Greek word is* chrestotes, *quite commonly translated* goodness *and sometimes* gentleness.
>
> *Again this verifies the integration of the inner character and the outward expression of our lives as we grow up into the full stature of Christ. We become patient and kind, good and gentle.*
>
> *The brightest facet on this diamond of kindness is suggested by the fact that old wine is called* chrestos *(mellow), and Christ's yoke is likewise called* chrestos *(Matt. 11:30). The yoke of Christ does not chafe or gall; it fits, it is easy. Does that not suggest a style of relationship, being with another in the way that Christ is with us, making the way of the other easier because we are yoked with them?*
> —Dunnam, *The Communicator's Commentary*, p. 118

What punch that puts into the world—kindness as an expression of Christ's presence within us. Thus it is a way of being with others that gives them the strength and power they need to go on.

In one of his sermons, Mark Trotter told the story about a young woman who lost her husband, a doctor, in India during the second World War. He died from some tropical disease. The shock of it sent her into despair. She lost all interest in life, not caring whether she lived or died. She booked passage on a ship back to

America and on that ship she met the survivor of another tragedy, a seven-year-old boy, whose missionary parents had been killed in the fighting in Burma. The little boy was attracted to the woman. A seven-year-old needs a mother, especially under those circumstances. But she would have nothing to do with him. In fact, she scheduled her time on shipboard so as to avoid him. She couldn't get outside herself and her sorrow long enough to comfort a little boy. "I have my own problems to deal with" is the way she put it.

The ship was torpedoed one night and began to sink slowly. The woman came out on deck, preparing herself to go down with the ship. She had no will to live and decided not even to seek an escape. But on the deck she saw the little boy, shivering with cold and fright. He saw her, ran over, and clung to her. Something came over her. She led him to one of the lifeboats; they both got in, and, for the next several days, until they were rescued, she held him. Her friends, looking back on that incident, say they don't know whether the woman saved the boy or the boy saved the woman.

Kindness—yoked together in a fashion that makes the way of another easier. Why are we so blind that we fail to see kindness as the salvation needed by so many? I was with a man recently,—a big man, macho, some would say—successful both in terms of professional recognition and material wealth. But that day he was like a little child as he poured out his pain and talked about how desperately he needed to be loved and held and yoked together in gentle kindness with his wife. We mistakenly think it is only the woman who needs that in a marriage? In the past three months alone, we have counseled in three threatened marital breakups where that is the desperate need of the man. This is true not only in marriage but in all relationships. People need to have someone with them in the fashion that Christ is with us, making their way easier because we are yoked with them.

It's a shame that some words lose their sharp edge. They don't carry the meaning or evoke the response inherent in their call upon our life. "Kindness" is that kind of word. We don't see it as an action word, but it is. This fruit of the Spirit is an aggressive and assertive kindness—reaching out to establish an easy yoking.

REFLECTING AND RECORDING

Write the names of the three kindest persons you know.

1.

2.

3.

Now beside the names of each of those persons write brief notes describing them. Why do you consider them kind?

Spend a couple of minutes considering this definition of kindness: yoked together in a fashion that makes the way of another easier.

Is there anyone with whom you are yoked together in that fashion? Name that person or persons.

Is there anyone with whom you need to be yoked together but are not? Name that person.

DURING THE DAY

Call on the phone, visit, or write a note to at least one of the "kindest" persons you named above, expressing your gratitude for them.

If you named someone with whom you need to be "yoked together," begin to cultivate kindness in relation to that person.

DAY FIVE

Kindness—A Matter of Discipline

Then the word of the LORD came to Zechariah, saying, "Thus says the LORD of hosts: 'Execute true justice, show mercy and compassion everyone to his brother. Do not oppress the widow or the fatherless, the alien or the poor. Let none of you plan evil in his heart against his brother.'" But they refused to heed, shrugged their shoulders, and stopped their ears so that they could not hear. Yes, they made their hearts like flint, refusing to hear the law and the words which the LORD of hosts had sent by His Spirit through the former prophets. Thus great wrath came from the LORD of hosts.

—Zechariah 7:8-12, NKJV

The little-known and little-read prophet of the Old Testament, Zechariah, heard and expressed the word of the Lord as it had come to prophets before him. He expressed that word succinctly: "Render true judgments, show kindness and mercy. . . do not oppress the widow, the orphan, the alien, or the poor." This word was given fresh and even more powerful expression in the New Testament, climaxing with Jesus' standards by which we would be judged: "Just as you did it to one of the least of these . . . you did it to me" (Matt. 25:40).

At the heart of Jesus' message was the word Zechariah heard from God, a call to show kindness and mercy.

Yesterday we gave brief consideration to how some words lose their sharp edge; kindness being one of those. We don't see kindness as an action word. It doesn't carry the meaning or evoke the response inherent in its call to life. For that reason, cultivating this fruit of the Spirit requires discipline . . . discipline that is in short supply in our culture.

Russell Gough, a professor of philosophy and ethics at Pepperdine University, wrote a newspaper commentary in the *Lafayette Journal and Courier* on Dennis Rodman, a basketball player for the Chicago Bulls, which makes the case.

Our lives do not ultimately flourish or self-destruct because of our personality traits but because of our habits of character. Habit, not personality, is destiny.

The distinction is crucial, even if it's not obvious, and can help shed light on the uncivil and disrespectful behavior that increasingly plagues our sports culture and our society in general.

Take for instance the pattern of incivility and disrespect displayed by

Chicago Bulls basketball star Dennis Rodman. His most recent act of infamy—kicking a cameraman between the legs—aroused this nation's moral indignation....

Rodman's incivility is not pathological. It's moral. His unethical behavior is not best explained in terms of a personality disorder, as if he were suffering from a psychological condition over which he had no control. On the contrary, not only does Rodman know what he's doing when he's uncivil but, contrary to widespread opinion, he's also ultimately in control of himself.... He chooses of his own will to act this way. He doesn't need psychoanalysis so much as he needs discipline, and especially self-discipline.

—Gough, February 11, 1997

To be sure, this is a dramatic case, but Rodman's action illustrates the need for self-discipline in our day-to-day lives. Kindness is not natural because we are basically selfish persons. It requires decision, time, energy, deliberate action. It costs because often to be kind to another requires giving up something for ourselves. It often requires going against the tide, and walking the road less traveled. According to a June 1997 article in *Sky* magazine, kindness of this type was shown in Newton, Pennsylvania "where one of the few Jewish families in this small community put a menorah in their front window for Hanukkah. The window was smashed and symbols of anti-Semitism were painted on the house. In a show of support, 25 of the family's Christian neighbors purchased menorahs and placed them in *their* front windows" (page 46.).

REFLECTING AND RECORDING

We don't often consider kindness as a social witness, certainly not as "social protest." Give some time to thinking about how individuals, or a group of persons, or a Christian congregation could make a powerful social witness by expressing kindness in these areas:

Race relations

AIDS victims and the homosexual community

What other areas come to mind?

Write a prayer, expressing your desire for discipline in showing kindness and mercy and your commitment to "the least of these."

DURING THE DAY

Observe the incivility around you today—the lack of kindness and mercy. Guard against going with that flow. Deliberately practice random acts of kindness.

DAY SIX

Good for Nothing— Good for Something

A good name is to be chosen rather than great riches, loving favor rather than silver and gold. The rich and the poor have this in common: the LORD is the maker of them all. A prudent man foresees evil and hides himself, but the simple pass on and are punished. By humility and the fear of the LORD are riches and honor and life. Thorns and snares are in the way of the perverse; he who guards his soul will be far from them. Train up a child in the way he should go, and when he is old he will not depart from it.

—Proverbs 22:1-6, NKJV

In Perry County, Mississippi, where I grew up, I often heard this description of a person: "He's a good-for-nothing _____." The last word might be a rather descriptive expletive but even without that kind of designation the word was always hard and had a terrible put-down impact. I've even heard parents address a child, "You good-for-nothing little rascal."

It is an illustration of the strange way we use words. But it is descriptive. We can be good for something or good for nothing.

There is a more serious problem with the word *good* in current usage. We have made it an almost nothing word in our vocabulary. In this culture we don't think seriously about goodness because we don't think seriously about morality. Who wants to be good? It's another witness to how words lose their power. Good, however, is a powerful word in scripture. Proverbs 22:1 teaches, "A good name is to be chosen rather than great riches." Another book of biblical poetry also proclaims, "Better a good name than costly oil" (Eccles. 7:1, NJB). Commenting on this verse, Rabbi William Silverman says:

> *Good oil flows downward, while a good name ascends. Good oil is transient, while a good name endures forever. Good oil is spent, while a good name is not spent. Good oil is bought with money, while a good name is free of cost. Good oil is applicable only to the living, while a good name is applicable to the living and the dead. Good oil can be acquired only by the rich, while a good name can be acquired by the poor and rich. The scent of good oil is diffused from the bedchamber to the dining hall, while a good name is diffused from one end of the world to the other.*
> —Silverman, p. 75

We need to recover the rich meaning of the word "goodness." The Greek word for goodness is *agathosune*, which is a strictly biblical word, not used in secular Greek. Paul used it in Romans 15:14: "I myself feel confident about you, my brothers and sisters, that you yourselves are full of *goodness*, filled with all knowledge, and able to instruct one another" (author's emphasis). The way he used the word in Ephesians 5:9 is instructive: "For the fruit of the light is found in all that is *good* and right and true" author's emphasis. He uses the word in his prayer for the Thessalonians: "To this end we always pray for you, asking that our God will make you worthy of his call and will fulfill by his power every *good* resolve and work of faith" (2 Thess. 1:11, author's emphasis).

The richness of this uniquely Christian word needs to be recovered. It is a goodness that is "good for something" and is the fruit of the Spirit in the life of a Christian. The New Testament scholars reminds us that the goodness Jesus expressed was both prophetic and pastoral. Jesus expressed *agathosune*, goodness, in cleansing the temple and driving out the money-changers. His goodness is expressing itself prophetically, demanding a change, requiring a response, bringing the fruit of the Spirit to fruition.

Jesus expressed *chrestotes*, kindness, to the sinning woman who crashed the party at Simon's house and anointed Jesus' feet. In this understanding goodness is *prophetic* and kindness is pastoral. What a challenging way to think about it.

But how often do we think of goodness as prophetic, as confrontive truth demanding a response, calling for change? Goodness, which is Christian, does that. We see a good person, one whose profession and performance are in harmony, and we take note. We are challenged by a "good" family we know who recently took a young teenager of a different race into their home because he was in a hopeless situation. We are challenged by the fact that this family's goodness shows. It is good for something. They are putting their commitment to the "least of these" into concrete expression.

We are challenged by a "good" couple we know who have recently set out on a deliberate path of simple living. They are intentionally sloughing off the "goods" of this world, all the added things that do not serve any ultimate purpose, in order that they may be good stewards of their resources and more effectively serve others.

Goodness is prophetic. We need both goodness and kindness. Someone has said that Jesus came to comfort the afflicted and afflict the comfortable. We need the kind of life that has such integrity in relation to Christ that those around us who are comfortable in their apathy, unconcern, and insensitivity will be afflicted by our very presence, and those who are afflicted by the pains and problems of life will be comforted by that same presence.

REFLECTING AND RECORDING

Do you know a person whose simple goodness is a challenge to you? Name and briefly describe that person.

Would anyone who is comfortable in apathy, unconcern, and insensitivity be afflicted by your presence? This is not a yes-or-no question. Spend some time contemplating your own life in light of this statement: We need the kind of life that has such integrity in relation to Christ that those around us who are comfortable in their apathy, unconcern, and insensitivity will be afflicted by our very presence; and those who are afflicted by the pains and problems of life will be comforted by that same presence.

DURING THE DAY

Continue your practice of random acts of kindness.

Be Holy as I Am Holy

"All great things are only a great number of small things that have been carefully collected together." I think of this word of François Fénelon when I think of goodness. Fénelon elaborates:

> *Great virtues are rare: the occasions for them are very rare; and when they do occur, we are prepared for them, we are excited by the grandeur of the sacrifice, we are supported either by the splendour of the deed in the eyes of the world or the self-complacency that we experience from the performance of an uncommon action. Little things are unforeseen; they return every moment, they come in contact with our pride, our indolence, our haughtiness, our readiness to take offense; they contradict our inclinations perpetually. We would much rather make certain great sacrifices to God, however violent and painful they might be, upon condition that we should be rewarded by liberty to follow our own desires and habits in the detail of life. It is, however, only by fidelity in little things that a true and constant love to God can be distinguished from a passing fervor of spirit.*
>
> —Fénelon, Day 100

Goodness has to do with fidelity to little things, attention to the desires and habits of our lives. All fruit of the Spirit has to do with our sanctification, our "going on to perfection," as Methodists would put it. Goodness is especially related to sanctification. Our sanctification is both a gift and something in which we participate. As we are justified by grace through faith, so also the fruit of the Spirit grows in us through faith—our sanctification is through faith.

But it is not a process in which we are passive. We are actively engaged, both in constantly yielding our lives to Christ and the Spirit working within, and, as we considered on Day Five of this week, in exercising our will to cultivate attitudes and express actions that are Christlike.

The fruit of goodness is related to our call to holiness. God issues the command:

> *The Lord spoke to Moses saying: "Speak to all the congregation of the people of Israel and say to them: You shall be holy, for I the Lord your God am holy. You shall each revere your mother and father, and you shall keep my sabbaths: I am the Lord your God.*

Do not turn to idols or make cast images for yourselves: I am the
LORD your God."

—Leviticus 19:1-4

Note that following the call to "be holy" in the scripture above, there are specific requisites of holiness listed: respect for parents, observance of the Sabbath, resisting idolatry; and, if you read on in the text, consideration for the poor and afflicted, honesty, justice, equality, truth, sexual purity, assistance to those being attacked or oppressed, and abstinence from vengeance. As we noted on Day 4 of Week 5, the list of requisites for holiness has as its centerpiece the commandment, "You shall love your neighbor as yourself" (vs. 18).

Throughout the passage, there is the recurring reminder: "I am the LORD." Goodness is essential because we are children of a sovereign God who is holy and who is Lord. Holiness is not an option for Christians. As Christians we should be distinctive in the way we do business, in the way we relate to others, in our attitude toward the poor and the oppressed, in the way we live together faithfully in marriage, in the way we use our money, in the priorities we set for our living.

> *A student of Torah came to his teacher and announced that, in*
> *his opinion, he was qualified for ordination as a rabbi. "What*
> *are your qualifications?" asked the sage. The student replied: "I*
> *have disciplined my body so that I can sleep on the ground, eat*
> *the grass of the field, and allow myself to be whipped three times*
> *a day."*
>
> *"See yonder white [donkey]," said the teacher, "and be mind-*
> *ful that it sleeps on the ground, eats the grass of the field, and is*
> *whipped no less than three times daily. Up to the present, you*
> *may qualify to be [a donkey], but certainly not a rabbi."*
>
> —Silverman, p. 74

Holiness—goodness permeating the whole of our life—is the telling mark of a Christian.

REFLECTING AND RECORDING

Spend just a minute or two reflecting on this truth: "It is . . . only by fidelity in little things that a true and constant love of God can be distinguished from a passing fervor of spirit."

The following is a test of what may be considered "little things." Move through the list slowly, considering how your fidelity in these things may mark your love of God.

- faithfulness to your spouse
- love and care of children
- kindness to friends and neighbors
- truthfulness and integrity in relationships
- dependability in your work
- refusal to gossip and undermine the reputation of another
- ongoing expression of love and care, however simple and limited, for the outsider, the poor, the oppressed
- valuing of all persons, despite race or social position.

All these concerns are related to holiness—God's call to be holy as God is holy. If holiness is primarily the constant love of God and fidelity to God in little things, how is your life of holiness? Write a prayer expressing your feelings, failures, desires, commitments in regards to this call for you to be holy.

DURING THE DAY

Continue your practice of random acts of kindness and consider how this activity is related to holiness.

GROUP MEETING FOR WEEK SEVEN

Introduction

You may have begun your discussion last week about possibilities for your group continuing to meet. We would suggest two possibilities. One, you could select two or three weeks of the workbook that were especially difficult or meaningful. Go through those weeks as an extension of your time together.

Two, you could decide that you are going to continue your group, using another resource. You may appoint two or three persons to bring a resource suggestion to the group next week.

If this workbook style is meaningful, there are a number of other workbooks in the series:

- *The Workbook of Living Prayer*
- *The Workbook of Intercessory Prayer*
- *The Workbook on Spiritual Disciplines*
- *The Workbook on Becoming Alive in Christ*
- *The Workbook on Coping as Christians*
- *The Workbook on the Christian Walk*
- *The Workbook on Christians Under Construction and in Recovery*
- *The Workbook on Loving the Jesus Way*
- *The Workbook on the Seven Deadly Sins*

Another possibility is for one or two persons to decide they will recruit and lead a group of persons through this workbook. Many people are looking for a small-group experience, and this is a way to respond to their need.

Sharing Together

1.   Spend three to five minutes "warming up" your sharing by asking persons to name in a brief sentence or two what kind of situations try their patience most. Reflect for a bit on what this says about you.

2.   Spend a few minutes getting patience into perspective by discussing the fact that the Greek word *makrothymise* is translated "forbearance" and "long-suffering" as well as "patience."

3.   On Day Two, you were asked to name persons who most often "get on your nerves" and try your patience. Then you were asked to reflect on what role *selfishness* plays in what these persons do to try you, as well as what role selfishness plays in making you impatient. Share honestly for five to eight minutes your experiences.

4.   Invite someone to read aloud Ed Wheat's word about divorce on page 149. How does the group respond to this? Take no more than five minutes.

5.   Invite a person or two to share an experience of being impatient with God. What can persons in the group learn from these sharings?

6.   Ask if any person would be willing to share an experience of being impatient with another person's weakness? What can persons in the group learn from their sharing?

7.   If the person who shared about being impatient with another person's weakness is willing, he might share his reflections on the question, "If you were God, how might you change in relation to the person you have been impatient with?"

8.   Spend a few minutes discussing kindness as being "yoked together in a fashion that makes the way of another easier." How have members of the group experienced that?

9. Spend five or six minutes talking about kindness as a social witness.

10. Invite two or three persons to describe persons whose simple goodness is a challenge to them.

11. Spend the balance of your time in this fashion. Turn to the Reflecting and Recording time on Day Seven. Let the leader read the list—stopping after each—spending time talking about how fidelity in each of these things marks our love of God.

PRAYING TOGETHER

We hope that your time together has made you "comfortable" in your praying together. Enter a "season of prayer" now by inviting two people to read the prayer they wrote during the Reflecting and Recording period of Day Five—a prayer expressing desire for discipline in showing kindness and mercy and your commitment to "the least of these."

Now begin a time of open prayer with any person in the group offering a few sentences of prayer about any concern. This may take on the structure of "conversational prayer." What one person prays will stimulate another to center his/her prayers. That means a person doesn't have to do all her praying at once. You may pray a sentence or two now about something that is on your heart. Later, someone else's prayers, or the direct leading of the Spirit, may stimulate you to verbalize other concerns.

Spend as much time as necessary in a "season of prayer," with different people praying as they will. You might then want to close by singing a chorus or a verse of a familiar hymn.

Week Eight

Faithfulness

Gentleness

Self-Control

Faith and Faithfulness

What then are we to say? Should we continue in sin in order that grace may abound? By no means! How can we who died to sin go on living in it? Do you not know that all of us who have been baptized into Christ Jesus were baptized into his death? Therefore we have been buried with him by baptism into death, so that, just as Christ was raised from the dead by the glory of the Father, so we too might walk in newness of life. For if we have been united with him in a death like his, we will certainly be united with him in a resurrection like his. We know that our old self was crucified with him so that the body of sin might be destroyed, and we might no longer be enslaved to sin. For whoever has died is freed from sin. But if we have died with Christ, we believe that we will also live with him. We know that Christ, being raised from the dead, will never die again; death no longer has dominion over him. The death he died, he died to sin, once for all; but the life he lives, he lives to God. So you also must consider yourselves dead to sin and alive to God in Christ Jesus.

—Romans 6:1-11

During Week Four, we gave a good bit of attention to faith as one of the three so-called "theological virtues." Today, let's think about faith and faithfulness; faithfulness being a fruit of the spirit.

When William Stringfellow died in March 1985 at the age of fifty-six, he was wellknown as a defender of the poor and unpopular causes lawyer, theologian, and author. Stringfellow was an outspoken opponent of all forms of oppression. He was one of the most outstanding lay theologians of this century. In 1974, he served as defense lawyer for the eleven women irregularly ordained to the Episcopal priesthood. This case opened the way for the recognized ordination of women in the Episcopal Church.

On March 5, three days after his death, friends and family of William Stringfellow gathered at his island home to celebrate his life. Daniel Berrigan, Roman Catholic priest, poet, and peace advocate, gave the eulogy at the memorial service that day. This is a part of what he said about William Stringfellow in a May 1985 issue of *Sojourner:*

168

For thousands of us, he became the honored keeper and guardian of the word of God; that is to say, a Christian who could be trusted to keep his word, which was God's word made his own. To keep that word close, to speak it afresh, to make it new. . . .

He could act honorably and courageously on occasion, in the breech, because he lived that way, over the long haul. In public and private, in good times and ill, in health and sickness, he kept his word.

And that word, which he kept and guarded and cherished, it now keeps him. That is the way with the Word, which we name Christ. The Covenant keeps us, who keep the Covenant."

—Berrigan, p. 33

That's the picture of faithfulness: "The Covenant keeps us who keep the Covenant." Because our faith is in God's faithfulness, we can be faithful.

Days like ours call for faith and faithfulness: faith in the One who, in all grace, died for our sins, and died that sin and evil might die; faithfulness to our experience of redemption and the promise that, by Jesus' power, "we might no longer be enslaved to sin" (Rom. 6:6).

Days like ours call for faithfulness. Political problems which are baptized with evil and energized by institutional selfishness are complex, some would say insoluble. Human problems such as poverty and starvation are so monumental that we're tempted to throw up our hands. The strong forces of evil have their work recorded in daily news stories of crime, pornography, violence, racism, human beings exploited and their dignity trampled in the mud of the ghetto. The word of Paul that sin abounds is an understatement. But Paul didn't stop with a partial diagnosis. "Sin abounds—but grace abounds even more." Hard to see! Oh yes! So very hard to see. And that's the reason the fruit of faithfulness is in great demand.

One example of such faithfulness is when civil war broke out in Albania in early 1997. Strife and violence pervaded every community. It was senseless and no one seemed to know who the enemy was. One young man, Mark Nyberg the director of an orphanage there, would not leave, however. Daily television news reported his story. Rather than flee the country, he moved into the orphanage and stayed with the children.

REFLECTING AND RECORDING

As much as we like to think, we don't just luck into things. The most meaningful things in life—our relationship to God, friendship, opportunities—come as a result of the decisions we have made, the steps we have taken.

Think about that in terms of your own life. Make some notes about where you are in life as a result of the steps you have taken. What role have faith and faithfulness played?

Spend a bit of time pondering this claim: *The Covenant keeps us who keep the Covenant.*

Describe an experience in your life when because of your faith in God's faithfulness, you were faithful. Make enough notes to bring the experience to life in your memory.

DURING THE DAY

As you move through this day, be deliberate in observation, conversation, attentiveness to the news, and to circumstances in your community. What are the human problems and social issues which call for the faithfulness of God's people in witness and service?

DAY TWO

While We Know the Worst, We Believe the Best

What then are we to say about these things? If God is for us, who is against us? He who did not withhold his own Son, but gave him up for all of us, will he not with him also give us everything else? Who will bring any charge against God's elect? It is God who justifies. Who is to condemn? It is Christ Jesus, who died, yes, who was raised, who is at the right hand of God, who indeed intercedes for us. Who will separate us from the love of Christ? Will hardship, or distress, or persecution, or famine, or nakedness, or peril, or sword? As it is written, "For your sake we are being killed all day long; we are accounted as sheep to be slaughtered." No, in all these things we are more than conquerors, through him who loved us. For I am convinced that neither death, nor life, nor angels, nor rulers, nor things present, nor things to come, nor powers, nor height, nor depth, nor anything else in all creation, will be able to separate us from the love of God in Christ Jesus our Lord.

—Romans 8:31-39

I never will forget an experience I had shortly after my decision to become a preacher. I went to a "Youth and Missions Conference" at Lake Junaluska, North Carolina. The featured speaker was John Havea from Tonga. John was then a relatively young man. He's now an elder statesman of the Methodist Church in the Pacific Islands. When I heard him years ago, he told the amazing story of John Hunt, a young Methodist missionary from England who helped to convert many people in the Tongan Islands who had been cannibals. John Hunt wrote in his journal about the stench of burning human flesh when the warriors returned from their raids and prepared for their feasts.

John Hunt continued to bear his witness bravely and patiently in that awful setting of human beings feeding on human beings. He died in 1848 with little sign of any general repentance or conversion. Then, some years after his death, the main chief, Thakombau, became a Christian and led a movement into the church.

I remember John Havea telling about a little church on one of the islands where there is a rough stone with the top hollowed out, used as a baptismal fount. He told us that was the old killing stone upon which Thakombau had killed his victims. It had been stained with human blood and the red stain was still there. Yet that stone for killing had become a fount for baptism.

The missionary John Hunt's faithfulness paid off. Today a large percentage of Tongans (at least eighty-five) and Fijians (fifty-three percent) are Christians.

"Sin abounds, yes, but grace abounds much more." That's hard to see, so very hard to see. But if God is for us, who can be against us? While we know the worst, we believe the best. As long as we have witnesses about killing stones becoming baptismal founts, we know to whom the ultimate victory belongs, and we can be faithful. And the more faithful we are, the greater the harvest of the Spirit in our lives will be.

REFLECTING AND RECORDING

Who is the person who comes most vividly to your mind when you think of faithfulness? Name and describe that person here.

Listed here are some categories of faithfulness. Give each some thought in terms of your own faithfulness in each of these areas.

Ministry

Christian values

Spouse and marriage vows

The church

Parents

Children

Now look at each area of faithfulness. Think of the persons you know who most vividly express faithfulness in each area, and write their name beside that category.

DURING THE DAY

Deliberately exercise faithfulness in ministry, Christian values, spouse and marriage vows, the church, as parents, as children. Where is the call most intense? Where are you most deficient?

DAY THREE

The Gentle Meek

There is a parallel between Jesus' beatitudes and Paul's list of the fruits of the Spirit. Spend a bit of time thinking about how the fruit match those characteristics Jesus called blessed.

Paul's fruits of the Spirit (Galatians 5:22-23): 1) love 2) joy 3) peace 4) patience 5) kindess 6) goodness 7) faithfulness 8) gentleness 9) self control.

Jesus' beatitudes (Matthew 5:3-11)

_____ Blessed are the poor in spirit, for theirs is the kingdom of heaven.

_____ Blessed are those who mourn, for they will be comforted.

_____ Blessed are the meek, for they will inherit the earth.

_____ Blessed are those who hunger and thirst for righteousness, for they will be filled.

_____ Blessed are the merciful, for they will obtain mercy.

_____ Blessed are the pure in heart, for they will see God.

_____ Blessed are the peacemakers, for they will be called children of God.

_____ Blessed are those who are persecuted for righteousness' sake, for theirs is the kingdom of heaven.

_____ Blessed are you when people revile you and persecute you, and utter all kinds of evil against you falsely on my account. Rejoice and be exceedingly glad, for your reward is great in heaven, for in the same way they persecuted the prophets who were before you.

The third beatitude, "Blessed are the meek," is Jesus' affirmation of the person who has the fruit of gentleness growing in her life. The Greek word here, *prautes*, is the most untranslatable of Paul's list. Barclay suggests that it is the adjectival form *praus* that throws most light on its meaning. This word is used to describe an animal who has been tamed and brought under control. For the Christian it means submission to the will of God. "Blessed are the meek," is talking about the kind of person who is faithful and submissive to God even in the midst of trial. The meekness, or gentleness, that is blessed by our Lord is not weakness; it is strength. The meek person is the person who knows his or her strength, but submits that strength to Christ in a ministry of love and caring for others. This kind of person Martin Luther described as "the most free lord of all."

In his second letter to Timothy, Paul talks about a "worker approved by God," one who has no need to be ashamed.

> *And the Lord's servant must not be quarrelsome but kindly to everyone, an apt teacher, patient, correcting opponents with gentleness. God may perhaps grant that they will repent and come to know the truth.*
>
> —2 Timothy 2:24-25

This description of a servant of the Lord illuminates specific aspects of meekness. One, *respectful of others*: "not quarrelsome but kindly." The gentle meek do not have to prove themselves. They don't build themselves up by tearing others down.

Two, *purposeful but person-centered*: "patient." The gentle meek have a purpose, a life-agenda that is clear, but they value persons more than process or prowess. They are willing to move more slowly if necessary to express value for persons.

Three, *certain and confident*, but not arrogant and proud: "correcting opponents with gentleness." The gentle meek know who they are and are strong in their convictions, but they don't use their strength to intimidate another.

REFLECTING AND RECORDING

Go back to the listing of the fruit of the Spirit and the beatitudes. Look at each fruit in relation to the beatitudes. Which beatitudes do they match most closely? Put the number of the fruit beside each beatitude it matches. For instance, in light of our consideration today, we would put a 4, a 5, and an 8 beside "Blessed are the meek."

DURING THE DAY

Take notice of the gentle, meek folks you meet today. Remember their characteristics: respectful of others, purposeful but person-centered, certain and confident but not arrogant and proud. Measure your own attitudes and encounters by these characteristics.

DAY FOUR

The Meek Are Not Weak

LORD, You have heard the desire of the humble; You will prepare their heart; You will cause Your ear to hear, to do justice to the fatherless and the oppressed, that the man of the earth may oppress no more.

—Psalm 10:17-18, NKJV

For yet a little while and the wicked shall be no more; indeed, you will look carefully for his place, but it shall be no more. But the meek shall inherit the earth, and shall delight themselves in the abundance of peace.

—Psalm 37:10-11, NKJV

Yesterday we noted that the Greek word for gentle or meek, *prautes*, is used to describe an animal who has been trained and brought under control. That's a very helpful image.

Evelyn Underhill used a sheepdog as a model for the Christian. She says that a well-trained sheepdog sits at his master's feet, looks him in the eye, never moving until he receives his command from the master. Then when that command is clear, he responds immediately, goes to do his master's bidding, and, in it all, never ceases to wag his tail.

For the Christian, to be meek means to be submissive to the will of God, and to find happiness in it. So meekness is not weakness as we have sometimes thought; it is strength. The meek know who they are. That's the source of their strength. They are not out to prove anything. They don't have to pretend.

Peter Ustinov is one of the great actors of our day. I don't know much about him, but I was impressed by a television interview some years ago during the filming of the movie *Death on the Nile*. He was talking about the images actors have to live with. An image is an awful thing, he said. An actor says, "I'm going to do this or that." And someone will say, "What about your image?" Ustinov said, "I don't know what my image is. I don't want to know." And then he continued, "It is a sad state when the man looking at you in a mirror is more important than the man looking into the mirror."

The meek are not caught in that bind. Because they don't pretend, they don't have to prove anything. They don't have to worry about their image.

The meek also know their need of God, and they never forget their story. We are reminded of Eleanor Boyer who won the New Jersey state lottery in November 1997. She was on the front page of *USA TODAY* because she secretly and suddenly gave all the money away. Explaining her generosity she simply said, "I have my pension and Social Security. I have everything I need. Why let the money sit in the bank till I die?" After her big win, she waited only three weeks before donating more than $5.9 million to her parish, The Church of the Immaculate Conception in Somerville, New Jersey. Keeping her generosity mainly local, she has also given to various charitable organizations, needy persons in her neighborhood, and three nephews who are her only close relatives. Even with the huge gift to her church, the interest on Eleanor's winnings—$10,000 a month—was coming in faster than she could give it away. She was deluged with letters and requests, each one getting personal attention and an immediate decision.

While she has always expressed a desire to remain private, there has been a great deal of publicity associated with Eleanor's generosity. Lottery officials and experts across the nation know of no one who has given away such a great amount, so quickly and so fully. Despite all the publicity, however, Eleanor Boyer's life has changed little. She remains in Somerville in the same gray Cape Cod-style house where she was born. And the church remains her focus as it has all her life. She has sung in the choir, taught religion classes, and counted the Sunday offering. She continues to attend Mass daily, driving her 1969 Chevy Malibu. She continues to rise early for prayer and to drop her weekly envelope in the collection plate. Rick Hampton, in this Good Friday article for *USA TODAY* wrote of Eleanor, "She heads down the street in her sensible old shoes. In this, the Christian season [Lent] of giving up, of going beyond, of emptying out, Eleanor Boyer looks like the richest woman in town."

Eleanor knows her need of God. She knows her story and she will never forget it. To be meek, we must remember our story. No matter what happens to us, how successful we are, to what level of accomplishment we may have risen, we remember the soil from which we have grown, those who have made us who we are. We know but for the grace of God we might be enslaved to some powerful addiction or entangled in the impossible bonds of a sick relationship.

REFLECTING AND RECORDING

Yesterday, we looked at the parallel between Jesus' beatitudes and the fruit of the Spirit. We mentioned earlier that some Bible scholars believe that love is the fruit of the Spirit, and the other fruit are expressions of love. Let's see how the fruit of the Spirit parallel the characteristics of love in 1 Corinthians 13. Put the numbers of the fruit of the Spirit beside the matching phrases Paul used to define love. 1) love 2) joy 3) peace 4) patience 5) kindess 6) goodness 7) faithfulness 8) gentleness 9) self control.

____ love is patient
____ love is kind
____ love is not envious or boastful or arrogant
____ or rude.
____ it does not insist on its own way
____ it is not irritable or resentful
____ it does not rejoice in wrongdoing, but
____ rejoices in the truth
____ it bears all things
____ it believes all things
____ it hopes all things
____ it endures all things

The following characteristics of the meek are listed here with a rating line, one to five, beside each. Rate yourself in relationship to these characteristics. How well do you know who you are and how secure are you in that? To what degree do you know your need of God? Do you remember your story? Do you stay in touch with from where you have come? One represents "very little or none"; five represents "very well." Put yourself on the bar of each characteristic.

I know who I am   1____2____3____4____5____
I know my need of God   1____2____3____4____5____
I never forget my story 1____2____3____4____5____

DURING THE DAY

Memorize the three affirmations: *I know who I am; I know my need of God; I never forget my story.* Repeat these affirmations as you move through the day, especially when you are tempted to be arrogant and self-assertive, rather than truly meek.

Self-Control—No Lasting Freedom and Joy without It

"All things are lawful," but not all things are beneficial. "All things are lawful," but not all things build up. Do not seek your own advantage, but that of the other. Eat whatever is sold in the meat market without raising any question on the ground of conscience, for "the earth and its fullness are the Lord's." If an unbeliever invites you to a meal and you are disposed to go, eat whatever is set before you without raising any question on the ground of conscience. But if someone says to you, "This has been offered in sacrifice," then do not eat it, out of consideration for the one who informed you, and for the sake of conscience—I mean the other's conscience, not your own. For why should my liberty be subject to the judgment of someone else's conscience? If I partake with thankfulness, why should I be denounced because of that for which I give thanks? So, whether you eat or drink, or whatever you do, do everything for the glory of God.
—1 Corinthians 10:23-31

The last fruit in the list is self-control.

The KJV translates this word, egkrateia, *as temperance. It is that, but more. It has to do with the mastery of the self. This is the Christian's overcoming of the "flesh-works" Paul has already listed. It is used both to refer to an athlete's discipline of his body and to the Christian's refusal to give free reign to impulse and desire.*

[In the scripture above,] Paul said that even when things are lawful and not harmful, they should be subjected to three

tests: Is it helpful? Is it constructive? Is it to the glory of God? (1 Corinthians 10:23, 31). If that principle is true of that which is not harmful and lawful, how much more should we ask those questions of those drives, desires, and impulses which we know play havoc with our physical health, our mental and spiritual well-being, our relationship with others?

The purpose of self-control is that we may be fit for God, fit for ourselves, and fit to be servants of others. No wonder Paul listed it as a fruit of the Spirit. Like all the other expressions, it too flows out of love. It is not a rigid religious practice—discipline for discipline's sake. It is not dull drudgery aimed at exterminating laughter and joy. It is the doorway to true joy, true liberation from the stifling slavery of self-interest and fear. In that sense it is bound to joy, for joy is the keynote of all disciplines aimed at self-control.

—Dunnam, pp. 119-120

A quotation by George MacDonald in *Christianity Today* provides challenging clarity.

Christ died to save us, not from suffering, but from ourselves; not from injustice, far less from justice, but from being unjust. He died that we might live—but live as he lives, by dying as he died who died to himself that he might live unto God. If we do not die to ourselves, we cannot live to God, and he that does not live to God, is dead.

—MacDonald, p. 45

Grace makes this possible. The command for holy living is accompanied by the offer of divine strength. I heard a seasoned lay Christian put it this way. "At first I thought the Christian life was easy. Only a few months had passed before I realized it was difficult. Finally, in my struggles and frustration, I discovered it was impossible." And then he added, "In my despair, I turned from my own self-efforts to Christ. I made the glorious discovery that living the Christian life is not my responsibility, but my response to Christ's ability."

REFLECTING AND RECORDING

Spend a bit of time reflecting on this claim: Living the Christian life is not my responsibility, but my response to Christ's ability.

What is the one area in your life where you need more self-control? Name that area here.

What is the special satisfaction you receive in allowing that area to be out-of-control?" Describe.

Is your lack of self-control in this area hurting you and others?

Is the satisfaction you receive from your lack of self-control worth the price you pay? Have you surrendered that area of your life completely to Christ?

Write a prayer confessing your lack of self-control, your inability to control your attitudes, passions, desires, actions, within your own strength. Rededicate yourself to Christ, and surrender this particular area of your life to Christ's "ability" and control.

DURING THE DAY

Stay aware of these three questions as you move through the day: Is it helpful? Is it constructive? Is it to the glory of God?

DAY SIX

The Harmony of Self-Control

For I handed on to you as of first importance what I in turn had received; that Christ died for our sins in accordance with the scriptures, that he was buried, and that that he was raised on the third day in accordance with the scriptures, and that he appeared to Cephas, then to the twelve. Then he appeared to more than five hundred brothers and sisters at one time, most of whom are still alive, though some have died. Then he appeared to James, then to all the apostles. Last of all, as to one untimely born, he appeared also to me. For I am the least of the apostles, unfit to be called an apostle, because I persecuted the church of God. But by the grace of God I am what I am, and his grace toward me has not been in vain. On the contrary, I worked harder than any of them—though it was not I, but the grace of God that is with me. Whether then it was I or they, so we proclaim and so you believe. Now if Christ is proclaimed as raised from the dead, how can some of you say that there is no resurrection of the dead?

—1 Corinthians 15: 3-12

One of the thoughts we considered yesterday is that the purpose of self-control is to be fit for God, to be fit for ourselves, and fit to be servants of others. That is a rather encompassing description of the Christian life. To help us in the process, we suggested three questions to ask ourselves of our drives, desires, impulses, actions and attitudes: Is it helpful? Is it constructive? Is it to the glory of God?

Coming from a slightly different direction, self-control is about three things:

1) deciding for ourselves the direction our lives will take;

2) knowing who we are, and staying in harmony with our "identity";

3) controlling our passions, rather than allowing our passions to control us.

On the surface, all of this seems to indicate no more than self-mastery, something that may have little or nothing to do with the Christian faith. Many philosophies of life call for discipline and self-control; certainly we would affirm this call no matter from which quarter it comes. Yet, Paul names "self-control" as a fruit of the Spirit. In his own life, he had discovered that self-mastery was a futile ideal apart from the empowerment of the indwelling Christ. We have referred often to his mournful confession: "For the good that I would I do not; but the evil which I would not, that I do. . . . O, wretched man that I am!" (Rom. 7:19, 24, NKJV).

Even though we may achieve a degree of self-mastery without the presence and power of the indwelling Christ, the likelihood is that it would make us into persons who stoically control ourselves but are without the liveliness, spontaneity, and joy of persons "alive in Christ." With this perspective, consider what self-control is all about.

First, *deciding for ourselves the direction our lives will take is the first step in developing self-control.* When we allow the Holy Spirit to grow in us the spirit of self-control, we can write our own story. We see the opposite happening with so many people. They are so other-dependent, so out of control of their own drives, passions, and impulses, that they are blown hither and yon by every wind of expectation coming from others.

Closely akin to this is a second factor: *knowing who we are, we can stay in harmony with our own identity.* My friend Emerson Colaw, who is a retired United Methodist bishop, tells the story of six-year-old Mary Taft of the famous Ohio political family. They were members of his congregation in Cincinnati. During Mary's first week at school, the teacher asked each of the students to introduce themselves and to tell something about their family. When it came little Mary's turn, she stood up and said, "I am Mary Taft. My great-grandfather was the President of the United States. My grandfather was a Senator, my father is a Congressman, and I am a Brownie!"

Would that all of us had and could keep that sort of confidence in our identity. The mark of self-control is that we can stay in harmony with our basic identity even though we pass through all sorts of changes in our lives. Circumstances and the expectations of others influence us, but do not determine who we are. Paul speaks a great word which we can make our own: "But by the grace of God I am what I am" (1 Cor. 15:10).

This does not mean we are not complex persons for we are. We do change. We experience all sorts of conversions and we take on new styles, but there is a center, a core of identity with which self-control enables us to stay in harmony. Paul put it this way:

> For though we walk in the flesh, we do not war according to the flesh. For the weapons of our warfare are not carnal but mighty in God for pulling down strongholds, casting down arguments and every high thing that exalts itself against the knowledge of God, bringing every thought into captivity to the obedience of Christ.
>
> —2 Cor. 10:3-5, NKJV

That's the ultimate in self-control: "bringing every thought into captivity to the obedience of Christ."

An orchestra provides a good metaphor. An orchestra is not simply a collection of musicians; it is a collection of musicians that become an orchestra by being in harmony. We may be a complexity of drives, passions, impulses-at times feeling like many persons. Self-control enables us to be not several people but complex persons in harmony with our "unique self."

As self-control as a fruit of the Spirit grows in us, we are able to control our passions, rather than allow our passions to control us. Anger, sex drives, fear, greed, the need for security, and many other passions are powerful drives in our lives. Any one of these passions is powerful enough to control if given reign. We have seen marriages destroyed by lust; otherwise powerful persons made impotent by fear; happiness and peace destroyed by greed. We have seen lives totally controlled by unchecked sex drives or the need for security completely gone awry.

Without a center around which to order our lives, there is no way to define the circumference, so our passions send us flying in all sorts of wild directions. For the Christian, the center is Christ and the new life he brings, life-giving, ever-growing expression to the fruit of the Spirit: love, joy, peace, patience, kindness, goodness, faithfulness, gentleness, and self-control.

REFLECTING AND RECORDING

Examine your self-control quotient by the criteria we have considered. To what degree is your self-control enabling you to decide for yourself the direction your life will take?

Is your present practice of self-control sufficient for you to stay in harmony with your "identity"—your true self?

Is the fruit of self-control growing so richly in your life that you are controlling your passions, rather than allowing your passions to control you?

Write a prayer expressing your feelings of confession, repentance, and commitment in relation to self-control.

DURING THE DAY

Take note today of any occasion where you need more self-control.

Day Seven

A Fabulous Oxymoron

And to the angel of the church in Smyrna write, "These things says the First and the Last, who was dead, and came to life: 'I know your works, tribulation, and poverty (but you are rich); and I know the blasphemy of those who say they are Jews and are not, but are a synagogue of Satan. Do not fear any of those things which you are about to suffer. Indeed, the devil is about to throw some of you into prison, that you may be tested, and you will have tribulation ten days. Be faithful until death, and I will give you the crown of life. He who has an ear, let him hear what the Spirit says to the churches. He who overcomes shall not be hurt by the second death.' "

—Revelation 2:8-11, NKJV

As we write this, our father and grandfather is in the hospital. He had a stroke and is paralyzed on his right side. His name is Murdock, but for some reason we affectionately call him Mutt. He is ninety years old.

I visited him four weeks ago. He had just gotten out of the hospital with a blood clot in his left leg. The doctors thought they would have to amputate. The arteries were so hardened they couldn't remove the clot and were fearful the leg would "die" for lack of blood. We had a wonderful visit. We talked about my mother who died two years ago. Tears came to his eyes as he said he missed her more every day. They had lived together as husband and wife for nearly seventy years.

We talked about his life and faith. He knew he had come through a death-threatening situation and was not yet "out of the woods." I asked him what he thought about his close call and was he ready. His eyes twinkled and he smiled slightly: "I've been praying that I would live to be a hundred, but if I go tomorrow, it's OK. The Lord has been good."

During my visit, I asked him to sing for me. That has always been a part of our visits as a family—especially while Mamma was living—singing the gospel songs that have nurtured their faith in the Baptist church to which they belonged. This time Mutt sang a portion of two songs. One song, "You Never Mentioned Him to Me," is about our failure to witness for Christ: "You passed me day by day, and you knew I was astray, but you never mentioned him to me." The other is "On Jordan's Stormy Banks I Stand." A part of that song goes:

> On Jordan's stormy banks I stand and cast a wishful eye
> to Canaan's fair and happy land, where my possessions lie.

It was obvious Mutt was reflecting on how faithful he had been in living the Christian life and sharing Christ with others He was also expressing his wistful longing to be reunited with my mother in "Canaan's fair and happy land." I thought of the tombstones in the little country church cemetery 150 yards up the hill from the house. My Mama's last words to Mutt are engraved on her stone: "I'll meet you." Already in place is his tombstone with his response: "I'll be there."

When we think of our father/grandfather and mother/grandmother, especially this last visit, we think of Revelations 2:10. "Be faithful unto death, and I will give you the crown of life." It is a fabulous oxymoron: *faithful to death—crown of life*. This is what this workbook journey has been about: the making of persons fit for this life as persons "in Christ," Kingdom people now, and fit for the eternal Kingdom.

Not all of us will live until ninety with a prayer to go for 100, but we can have a twinkling eye—confidence that we if we go tomorrow, all will be well.

Dietrich Bonhoeffer was a German pastor and theologian during the rise of Hitler's Third Reich. From the beginning he sensed the evil of this rise of Nazi power and risked everything in his fight against it. In 1943 he was arrested and imprisoned in Berlin and later in Buchenwald. From prison he wrote letters that still define and call us to courage and hope. In one of his letters he shared this prayer: "Give me the hope that will deliver me from fear and faintheartedness." He was given that hope, which delivered him from fear and faintheartedness, and empowered him to face execution with courage.

Whatever happens, faithfulness and hope give us the confidence that God is alive and is sovereign.

The resurrection of Jesus provides that confidence and hope. I haven't visited Mutt since his stroke. He can't speak plainly. I talk to him through my sisters in his hospital room each day. I've told him how much I love him and what a good Daddy he has been. The chances are he may never sing again, but if he does, I'm sure it will be songs of faith and hope. We pray that this workbook journey has clarified the song of your life and given you confidence to sing it.

REFLECTING AND RECORDING

Go back to the beginning of the workbook and thumb through the pages. Spend as much time as you have being reminded of some of the most meaningful times you have had in this workbook journey.

DURING THE DAY AND ALL COMING DAYS

Remember Jesus' promise: "Be faithful unto death, and I will give you the crown of life."

GROUP MEETING FOR WEEK EIGHT

Introduction

This is the last meeting designed for this group. You have already talked about the possibility of continuing to meet. You should conclude those plans.

Whatever you choose to do, it is usually helpful to determine the actual time line in order that persons can make a clear commitment. Assign some persons to follow through with whatever decisions are made.

Your sharing during this session should reflect on the entire eight-week experience. (Leader: Save enough time to respond to suggestion 9.) Begin with your workbook experience this past week.

Sharing Together

1. Spend eight to ten minutes having persons share how they view where they now are in life as a result of decisions they have made and the way they have lived. What role has faith and faithfulness played in it?

2. Invite a person or two to share an experience when, because of faith in God's faithfulness, they were able to be faithful.

3. Invite two people to name and describe the person that comes vividly to their minds when they think of faithfulness.

4. On Day Three, Paul's fruits of the spirit are listed in parallel to Jesus' beatitudes. Spend five to eight minutes discussing how these match.

5. Ask this question, inviting the group to respond: What new insight or challenge did you receive this week as it relates to your understanding of meekness?

6. Invite one or two persons to name and describe a person who fits this description: "The meek know who they are. That's their source of strength. They are not out to prove anything. They don't have to pretend."

7. Invite one or two persons to name and describe a person who is meek because he knows his need of God or because she never forgets her story.

8. Spend six to nine minutes discussing that self-control is about three things: deciding for ourselves the direction our lives will take; knowing who we are, and staying in harmony with our "identity"; and controlling our passions, rather than allowing our passions to control us.

Keep the discussion personal and confessional. How are these dynamics operating in your life?

9. Take twelve to eighteen minutes with persons sharing what these eight weeks have meant to them—new insights, challenges, things they need to work on in their lives.

Praying Together

1. Begin your time of prayer by asking each person briefly to express gratitude to God for something significant that has happened to him or her as a result of these eight weeks.

2. Give each person an opportunity to share whatever decision or commitment he or she has made, or will make in relation to Christ and cultivating virtue and the fruits of the Spirit. It is important that these be specific. Follow each person's verbalizing of these decisions and commitments by having another person in the group offer a brief prayer of thanksgiving and support for that person.

3. A benediction is a blessing or greeting shared with another, or by a group, in parting. The "passing of the peace" is such a benediction. You take a person's hand, look into his or her eyes, and say, "The peace of the Lord be with you" and receive the response, "And also with you." Standing in a circle, let the leader "pass the peace," and let it go around the circle.

4. Having completed the passing of the peace, speak to one another in more spontaneous ways. Move about to different persons in the group, saying whatever you feel is appropriate for your parting blessing to each person. Or you may simply embrace the person and say nothing. In your own unique way, "bless" each person who has shared this journey with you.

BIBLIOGRAPHY

Alter, Margaret Gramatky. "The Unnatural Act of Forgiveness." *Christianity Today* (June 16, 1997).

Campbell, Will D. *Brother to a Dragonfly.* New York: The Continium Publishers Corporation, 1995.

Carney, Mary Lou. *Spiritual Harvest.* Nashville: Abingdon Press, 1987.

Coles, Robert. *The Story of Ruby Bridges.* New York: Scholastic Inc., 1995.

Dunnam, Maxie D. *The Communicator's Commentary Series, Volume 8: Galatians, Ephesians, Philippians, Colossians, Philemon.* Waco, Texas: Word Books, Publisher, 1982.

Eiseley, Loren. *The Immense Journey.* Quoted in Robert A. Raines, *Creative Brooding.* New York: The Macmillan Company, 1966.

Fénelon, François. Quoted in John Baillie, *A Diary of Readings.* New York: Charles Scribner's Sons, 1955.

Goodman, Ellen. *The Hattiesburg American*, March 1, 1997, sec. 13A.

Gough, Russell. "Rodman's bad habit is morality question." *Lafayette Joural & Courier* (February 11, 1997).

Hampton, Rick. "Eleanor Boyer's generosity provides inspiration for many." *USA TODAY* (April 4, 1998).

Harper, Timothy. "Sistah Preaz." *Sky*, Delta Air Lines (June 1997).

Hobbs, Thomas. Quoted in Peter Thomas Geach, *The Virtues: The Stanton Lectures 1973-4.* Cambridge: Cambridge University Press, 1977.

Hughes, Selwyn. *How to Live the Christian Life.* New York: Seabury Press, 1982.

Jones, W. Paul. "Courage as the Heart of Faith." *Weavings: A Journal of the Christian Spiritual Life* 12, no. 3 (May/June 1997).

Lucado, Max. *In The Grip of Grace.* Dallas: Word Publishing, 1996.

MacDonald, George. *Unspoken Sermons* in *Christianity Today* (June 16, 1997).

Morris, Colin. *The Hammer of the Lord*, London: Epworth Press, 1973.

Niebuhr, Reinhold. *The Irony of American History.* Quoted in John Bartlett, *Familiar Quotations*. Boston: Little Brown Company, 1992.

Ortberg, John. *Christianity Today* (May 19, 1997).

Pascal. Blaise. Quoted in John Baillie, *A Diary of Readings.* New York: Charles Scribner's Sons, 1955.

Sanderson, John W. *The Fruit of the Spirit.* Grand Rapids, Mich. Zondervan, 1972.

Shoemaker, H. Stephen. *The Jekyll and Hyde Syndrome: A New Encounter with the Seven Deadly Sins and Seven Lively Virtues.* Nashville, Tenn.: Broadman Press, 1987.

Silverman, William B. *Rabbinic Stories for Christian Ministers and Teachers.* New York: Abingdon Press, 1958.

Smedes, Lewis B. *A Pretty Good Person.* San Francisco: Harper & Row, 1990.

Stewart, James S. *A Faith to Proclaim.* New York: Scribner's Sons, 1953.

The Louisville Times, July 13, 1984, sec. A16, as cited in H. Stephen Shoemaker, *The Jekyll & Hyde Syndrome.*

Wheat, Ed. *Love Life.* Grand Rapids, Mich.: Zondervan Publishing House, 1980.

O Love that wilt not let me go,
I rest my weary soul in thee;
I give thee back the life I owe,
That in thine ocean depths its flow
May richer, fuller be.

—George Matheson

For you make me glad by your deeds,
O LORD; I sing for joy at the works of your
hands.

—Psalm 92:4, NIV

And my God will fully satisfy every
need of yours according to his riches in
glory in Christ Jesus. To our God and
Father be glory forever and ever. Amen.

—Philippians 4:19-20